GREAT TEAMS, PLAYERS, & COACHES

Stories about high school basketball from the state of Illinois

by

Donald Brown M.S.

authorHOUSE®

AuthorHouse™
1663 Liberty Drive, Suite 200
Bloomington, IN 47403
www.authorhouse.com
Phone: 1-800-839-8640

First published by AuthorHouse   2/11/2009

ISBN: 978-1-4389-3718-2 (sc)

Printed in the United States of America
Bloomington, Indiana

This book is printed on acid-free paper.

PREFACE

The Marrilac House, Dr. Martin Luther King Jr. Boys Club, Navy Pier, Henry Horner Boys Club, Gladstone playground, and Our Lady of Sorrows were some of my favorite places to hone my basketball skills. Growing up playing basketball in Chicago were fun times. Basketball can be found in playgrounds, YMCA's, recreation centers, schools and clubs all over the city. It's inexpensive to play basketball, so I guess that's why it's called the city game.

I played basketball at Chicago (Crane) in the 1972 state final tournament. It was the state's highest scoring tournament and the state's first Class AA boys basketball tournament. Prior to that tournament, boys state basketball in Illinois was a single class tournament. We lost to Quincy in the quarterfinals 87-71, and Thornridge won the championship that year. In fact, Thornridge had a great team that year, ousting Quincy 104-69 in the title game.

Arguably, two of the best basketball teams in Illinois state schoolboy history were the Dolton (Thornridge) (33-0) 1972 state championship team and the Quincy (Sr.) (33-0) 1981 state championship team. Thornridge had an average point spread of 27 on its three elite eight games in 1972, and no opponent came closer than 14 points the entire season. On the other hand, after Quincy defeated Proviso East 68-39 for the title in 1981, they had won its Sweet Sixteen games by 28, 25, 31, and 29 points. Quincy was named No.1 in the nation.

Although there have been other great teams worthy of being mentioned in the same breathe with those two teams, measuring up against those two teams would be difficult. Thornridge had won the state championship the previous year too, and a then state record 58 consecutive victories. Quincy's Class AA state-record of 64 wins ended in the 1982 state championship against Chicago (Mendel) in the semifinals. Determining the best schoolboy players in Illinois, however, is far more difficult.

While growing up in Chicago, Billy Harris (Dunbar), Sammy Puckett (Hales Franciscan), and Quinn Buckner (Thornridge) were the most fun to watch, in my opinion. Other player that I've heard stories about while growing up in Chicago where; Cazzie Russell (Carver), Kevin Porter (DuSable), Jerome Freeman (Crane), Jim Brewer (Proviso East), Tom Kivisto (East Aurora), Marcus Washington (LaGrange), and Lloyd Batts (Thornton). When I played high school basketball on the West Side at Crane some of the players that I enjoyed watching was Lee Arthur Scott (Gordon Tech), Bo Ellis (Parker), Rickey Green (Hirsch), Sonny Parker (Farragut), Nate Williams (Crane) Lloyd Walton (Mt Carmel), James Jackson (Crane), and Arthur Sivels (Crane).

Obviously, since those days there have been many other entertaining basketball players and teams from the state of Illinois. Isiah Thomas (St Joseph), Mark Aguirre (Westinghouse), and Jay Shidler (Lawrenceville) are a few of the great players. Chicago (Simeon), Chicago (King), and Maywood (Proviso East) are some of the other great teams.

CONTENTS

APPENDICES

CHAPTER ONE

ILLINOIS HIGH SCHOOL ASSOCIATION

The Illinois High School Association (IHSA) is one of 52 state high school associations in the United States, designed to regulate competition in most interscholastic sports and some interscholastic activities at the high school level. It is a charter member of the National Federation of State High School Association (NFHS). The IHSA regulates 14 sports for boys, 14 sports for girls, and eight co-educational non-athletic activities. More than 760 public and private high schools in the state of Illinois are members of the IHSA. The Association's offices are in Bloomington, Illinois. In its over 100 years of existence, the IHSA has been at the center of many controversies. Some of these controversies (inclusion of sports for girls, the inclusion of private schools, drug testing, and the use of the term "March Madness") have had national resonance, or paralleled the struggles seen in other states across the country. Other controversies (geographic advancement of teams to the state playoff series, struggles between small schools and large schools, particular rules unique to Illinois competition) are more of a local focus.

GOVERNANCE

The IHSA is governed according to the rules of its constitution. The constitution covers the broadest policies of the Association, such as membership, governance, officers and their duties, and meeting requirements. The IHSA is led by an eleven-member Board of Directors. All eleven members are high school principals from member schools. Seven of the ten are elected to three-year terms from seven geographic regions within the state of Illinois. Three other board members are elected at-large. A treasurer, who does note vote, is appointed by the Board. The Board of Directors determines IHSA policies and employs an executive director and staff. They also work with the Illinois General Assembly, the Illinois State Board of Education, the Illinois Principals Association, the Illinois Association of School Boards, the Illinois Association of School Adminisrators, the Illinois Athletic Directors Association and the North Central Association.

The IHSA also has a 35-member Legislative Comission, consisting of 21 high school principals, seven high school athletic directors elected from each of the seven state regions, and seven at-large members. The commission reviews amendment proposals to the IHSA Constitution and By-Laws, and determines which are passed on to a vote of the member schools. Each school receives one vote on any amendments, with the voting taking place annually in December. Changes are passed by simple majority of member schools.

The day-to-day running of the association is charged to an administrative staff of nine, one of whom acts in the position of Executive Director. This group is directly responsible for setting up and running individual state playoff series in each sport and activity. They also supervise annual meetings with advisory committees from each sport and activity to review possible changes in the rules. They also coordinate committees on issues from sportsmanship and sports medicine to media relations and corporate sponsorship.

Subordinate to the Constitution and By-Laws are a number of policies. These policies are generally of greater interest to the public, as they more specifically deal with issues that affect the day-to-day operation of sports and activities. Examples of policies include individual athlete eligibility, rules governing the addition of new sports and activities, the classification of schools (1A, 2A, 3A, etc) and media relations. The key policy that has been a cornerstone of the IHSA is its policy on grouping and seeding tournaments. *The State Series is designed to determine a State Champion. The State Series is not intended to necessarily advance the best teams in the state to the State Final.* The IHSA is built upon the concept of geographic representation in its state playoff series.

HISTORY

EARLY YEARS

The IHSA was founded on December 27, 1900 at a rump session of the Illinois Principals Association. Known as the Illinois High School Athletics Association for the first 40 years of its existence, the IHSA is the second oldest of the 52 state high school associations. Only the Wisconsin Interscholastic Athletic Association outdates it, by two years.

For the greater part of a decade, the IHSA was concerned mostly with establishing school control over interscholastic athletic programs and setting eligibility standards for competition. Ringers were a persistent problem, and among schoolboy sports, football was a special concern. In this period, severe injuries and even deaths weren't uncommon, and there was much talk of banning football completely.

In 1908, the IHSA's mission expanded in an unforeseen direction when its board was convinced by Lewis Omer of Oak Park and River Forest to sponsor a statewide basketball tournament. Although a handful of other state associations had sponsored track meets, none had ever attempted to organize a statewide basketball tournament. The first tournament, an 11-team invitation held at the Oak Park YMCA was a financial success. Subsequent state tournaments, which were open to all member schools, provided the IHSA with fiscal independence, an important new vehicle to spread its message, and ever-increasing name recognition among the public.

By 1922, the affairs of the Association became so time-consuming that its board hired a full-time manager, Charles W. Whitten. As vice president of the Board, Whitten had recently reorganized the basketball tournament and reduced the size of the state finals from 21 teams to four. About the same time, the IHSA became a charter member of the National Federation of State High School Associations. In addition, to his IHSA responsibilities, Whitten ran the business affairs of the NFHS, at first unofficially, and after 1927 with the official title of general manager.

From this dual stage, Whitten and his assistant manager at IHSA, H.V. Porter, exerted unusual influence over high school sports, not only in Illinois, but across the nation. In one memorable battle, Whitten took on the "grand old man" of college football Amos Alonzo Stagg of the University of Chicago and effectively shut down his national tournament for high school basketball champions. Porter served on several NFHS committees and helped develop the molded basketball and the fan-shaped backboard, among other inventions. Porter later became the first full-time executive of the NFHS.

Of the many challenges that faced Whitten during his 20 year career, the one with the longest-lasting repercussions was the reorganization of 1940. Prior to this time, two large groups of Illinois high schools remained outside of IHSA controls: private school, which were not eligible for membership, and the public schools of Chicago, which were eligible for membership but had joined only sporadically. The new constitution approved in 1940 extended the privileges of membership to non-public schools and gave limited autonomy to the Chicago schools, which subsequently joined in masses. In addition, non-athletic activities such as speech and music were added to the IHSA's menu, prompting the elimination of the word "Athletic" from the Association's name.

As the Association matured, member schools requested sponsorship of state tournaments in sports other than basketball. The first such move came in 1927, when the IHSA took control of the Illinois Interscholastic, a festival of high school track, golf, and tennis run by the University of Illinois. The meet continued to be held on the campus in Champaign-Urbana, but as with basketball, IHSA involvement opened the field to all IHSA member schools and removed non-member schools, including a handful of out-of-state schools. The IHSA subsequently established state series in several other boys' sports: swimming and diving (1932), wrestling (1937), baseball (1940), cross country (1946), and gymnastics (1958) (gymnastics ha a University of Illinois sponsored state meet from 1952 through 1957). Few of those series were self-supporting, but the basketball tournament - sometimes referred to as the "goose that laid the golden egg" - paid the freight for all.

RECENT TIMES

While the mundane tasks of regulating eligibility and licensing remain just as important to the IHSA's mission as they were in the beginning, high-profile issues having to do with state tournaments - and who win them - have repeatedly stolen the spotlight in recent years. First of all, Illinois was one of the last states, and certainly the largest, to retain a one-class system where all schools, regardless of enrollment competed for the same prize. In December 1970 the smaller schools, who make up a majority of IHSA members, forced a binding referendum on whether to implement a two-class system in boys basketball, and the measure carried a narrow margin, 312-293. After this move, several other sports adopted the two-class format. In January 2006, after a substantial majority of schools responding to an advisory referendum indicated a preference for more classes, the IHSA Board of Directors approved expansion in several sports, starting in 2007-08.

At the culmination of the first drive for expansion, the IHSA also sought a way to add a state championship in football to its schedule of events. Because of the sheer number of schools involved, a playoff involving all member schools was not possible. In 1074, the IHSA introduced a five-class system in which teams qualified based on their regular-season performance. The addition of the football playoff coaxed the last large group of non-members, the schools of the Chicago Catholic League to join the IHSA. The playoffs were expanded to six classes in 1980 and eight classes in 2001.

The success of non-public schools in IHSA tournaments in recent years has led to considerable debate among the members, 83% of which are public schools. Although statistical studies seemed to indicate that, as a whole, non-public (and certain non-boundaried public schools) enjoy a disproportionate amount of success, there was little agreement on the reason. In 2005, the Board of Directors implemented a multipier for classification purposes that boosted the enrollments of non-boundaried schools by a factor of 1.65. A group of 37 private schools later sued the Association, and a settlement was reached that required the multplier to go through the Association's annual legislative process. In December 2005, the member schools voted 450-143 to retain the 1.65 multiplier.

Another lawsuit drew national attention in the 1990s, when the IHSA laid claim to "March Madness." The phrase was first used to describe the IHSA basketball tournament in an essay written by H.V. Porter in 1939 and published in the IHSA's monthly magazine. Over time the phrase came to be used for high school basketball tournaments, particularly in Illinois, but was not trademarked by the IHSA. When a television production company sought to register the phrase, the IHSA sued, leading to a battle that eventually involved the NCAA as well. In the end, a district court judge ruled that both the IHSA and NCAA could register the trademark and use the phrase for their own purposes. In addition, the IHSA is the sole owner of the mark, "America's Original March Madness."

On November 1, 2007, the Illinois Press Association (IPA) and two newspapers (the Northwest Herald and the State Journal-Register) filed for a temporay restraining order to prohibit the IHSA from enforcing its policy restricting the use of photographs taken at its state final events. The IHSA's policy, similar to those adopted by the NCAA, colleges such as Illinois State University and the University of Illinois, and other state high school associations, allows news-gathering organizations to sell photos that are published but prohibits the sale (usually through a website) of the many photos taken at the event that are not published. A circuit court judge denied the motion on November 5 and encouraged the parties to renew talks to resolve the impasse. The plainiffs withdrew their request for a preliminary injunction on November 16 as talks continued.

On December 5, 2007, the IHSA announced that it had filed a countersuit to the IPA seeking resolution to the ongoing issue, citing a failure on the part of the IPA to continue talks, and the ongoing sales of photographs. In January, 2008, it was announced that State Representative Joseph Lyons had submitted Illinois House Bill 4582, which would prevent the IHSA from enforcing its ban on press outlets from selling pictures of IHSA events.

On January 14, 2008, the IHSA announced that based on a survey of 54% of its principals, it would move forward to design and implement a program to test for the presence of performance-enhancing drugs in student athletes participating in select State Series competitions. While details have not been worked out, based on the vote of the principals, the membership would not favor forcing a team to forfeit in the event of a positive test. Further, the membership also voted overwhelmingly favored to support a period of ineligibility for athletes testing positive, and narrowly supported forcing schools to adopt education programs if an athlete tested positive.

EXECUTIVE DIRECTORS

Prior to 1991, this office was known as Manager or Executive Secretary.

- Charles W. Whitten, 1922-1942
- Albert Willis, 1942-1968
- Harry Fitzhugh, 1968-1978
- Lavere L. (Liz) Astroth, 1978-1991
- H. David Fry, 1991-2002
- Martin L. Hickman, 2002-present

NOTABLE MEDALIST IN IHSA SPONSORED STATE SERIES

- Dave Butz (Maine South H.S.) - professional football player - won the 1968 state championship in the discus.
- Bart Conner (Niles West H.S.) - Olympic athlete medaled 13 times between 1973 and 1975, including three State Titles on the parallel bars, and two All-Around State Titles.
- Jimmy Connors (Assumption H.S., East St. Louis) - international tennis star - placed fifth at the 1967 State Tennis Championship Tournament.
- Roger Ebert (Urbana H.S.) - film critic - won 1958 state title in radio speaking (Individual Events).
- Red Grange (Wheaton H.S.) - professional football player - medaled seven times in Track & Field (1920-22) including state championships in the high jump, 100 yard dash, long jump, and 220 yard dash.
- Dennis Hastert - Congressman and 59th Speaker of the U.S. House of Representatives - Head Wrestling Coach for Yorkville H.S. who won the 1976 Class A State Wrestling Championship.

- Edwin Hubble (Wheaton H.S.) - astronomer - won 1906 state championship in the high jump.
- Jackie Joyner-Kersee (Lincoln H.S., East St. Louis) - Olympic athlete - won five medals from 1978 to 1980, including individual state championships in the 440 yard dash, and the long jump (twice).

NATIONAL HIGH SCHOOL HALL OF FAME INDUCTEES

Twenty-two Illinoisans are members of the National High School Hall of Fame sponsored by the NFHS. The honorees, and their year of induction:

- H.V. Porter (1982), IHSA and NFHS administrator, coined the term "March Madness"
- Norman Geske (1982), official
- Arthur Trout (1982), coach
- Dwight (Dike) Eddleman (1983), athlete (football, basketball, athletics)
- Clifford Fagan (1983), NFHS administrator
- Vergil Fletcher (1983), coach
- Milton Sprunger (1983), IHSA administrator
- Fred (Brick) Young (1983), official
- Harold (Red) Grange (1984), athlete (football)
- Bart Conner (1986), athlete (gymnastics)
- John Griffith (1986), contributor
- Charles Farina (1987), coach (wrestling)
- Quinn Buckner (1989), athlete (basketball)
- Gordon Gillespie (1989), coach (wrestling)
- Jackie Joyner-Kersee (1989), athlete (athletics)
- Keith Parker (1990), official
- Dave Robertson (1991) coach
- William (Red) Schmitt (1993), coach
- Tom Frederick (1994), IHSA administrator
- Ola Bundy (1996), IHSA administrator
- Larry Wilcoxen (2002), official
- Joe Newton (2004), coach (cross country)

LIST OF IHSA MEMBER CONFERENCES

The following is a list of Illinois High School Association member conferences. Schools that belong to these conferences compete with each other on a local level in athletics and non-athletic activities.

- Apollo Conference
- Bi-County Conference
- Big Northern Conference (contains two divisions)
- Big Twelve Conference

- Black Diamond Conference
- Cahokia Conference (contains two divisions)
- Central State Eight Conference
- Central Suburban League (contains two divisions)
- Chicago Catholic League (contains two divisions)
- Chicago Prep Conference
- Chicago Public High School League (contains ten divisions)
- Corn Belt Conference
- DuPage Valley Conference
- East Suburban Catholic Conference
- Egyptian Illini Conference
- Four Rivers Conference
- Fox Valley Conference (contains two divisions)
- Girls Catholic Athletic Conference
- Greater Egyptian Conference
- Illini Central Conference
- Independent School League
- Inter County Athletic Conference
- Interstate Eight Conference
- Lincoln Trail Conference
- Little Illini Conference
- Little Seven Conference (1921-1995)
- Little Ten Conference
- Metro Suburban Conference (started during 2006-2007 academic year)
- Metropolitan Prep Conference
- Mid-Illini Conference
- Mid-South Conference
- Mid-State Conference
- Mid-Suburban Conference (contains two divisions)
- Midland Trail Conference
- Mississippi Valley Conference
- MSM
- National Trail Conference
- NCIC (North Central Illinois Conference - contains two divisions)
- New Salem Conference
- North Suburban Conference (contains two divisions)
- Northern Illinois Conference (NIC-10)
- Northwest Upstate Illini Conference (contains two divisions)
- Okaw Valley Conference
- Olympic Conference
- Pike County Conference
- Prairie State Conference
- Prairieland Conference
- Private School Conference
- River Valley Conference

- Sangomo Conference
- Sangomo Valley Conference (contains two divisions)
- SICA (South Inter-Conference Association, contains five divisions)
- South Central Conference (contains two divisions)
- South Egyptian Conference
- South Seven Conference
- South Suburban Blue
- Southern Illinois River-to-River Conference (with Mississippi and Ohio River divisions)
- Southwest Prairie Conference (started during 2006-2007 academic year)
- Suburban Catholic Conference
- Suburban Prairie Conference (contains three divisions)
- Three Rivers Conference
- Tollway Athletic Conference
- Tomahawk Conference
- Tri-County Conference
- Upstate Eight Conference
- West Central Conference
- West Suburban Conference (contains two divisions)
- Western Big Six Conference
- Western Illinois Valley Conference (contains two divisions)
- Western Sun Conference (started during 2006-2007 academic year)

CHAPTER TWO

CHICAGO HIGH SCHOOL BASKETBALL

CHICAGO PUBLIC HIGH SCHOOL LEAGUE

The Chicago Public High School Athletic Association, or commonly, known as the Chicago Public League (CPL), is the interscholastic competition arm of the Chicago Public Schools. The governance of the CPL is set through the Department of Sports Administration and Facilities of CPS. With over 70 high schools city-wide participating in at least one sport, the CPL is the largest autonomous athletic league of any age level - high school or older - in the world.

HISTORY

THE COOK COUNTY YEARS: 1900-1914

The origins of the Chicago Public League can be traced back to its predecessor, the Cook County High School League, which started in 1900. Some of the schools that participated in the Cook County League still exists today; Lane, Englewood, Hyde Park, Calumet, Austin, and Lake View. Two other schools from this league have since gone to other leagues around the area. Lyons High is now Lyons Township of LaGrange, which plays in the West Suburban Conference, as does Oak Park, now called Oak Park-River Forest.

THE CPS YEARS: 1914 AND BEYOND

When the Chicago Public League was formed in 1914, it brought the aforementioned schools from the disbanded Cook County League into the fold and added a few more, some of which are no longer in existence. The schools from the early days of the then North Side dominated CPl include McKinley, Tuley (now Clemente), and Parker (now Robeson). Also, some of the schools that remain today from the early years still exist. Those schools include Crane, Marshall, Fenger, Kelly, Kelvyn Park, Morgan Park, Wells, Tilden, Farragut, Senn, Manley, Schurz, Von Steuben, Chicago Vocational and South Shore. As the years rolled on, more schools were added to the roster, but until the 1940s, was a primarily all-Caucasian league.

With the Great Migration coming into play, more schools south of Madison Avenue started appearing, among those New Phillips (started as South Division and is now DuSable), Dunbar, Forrestville (now Martin Luther King), Simeon,

Carver, and later into the second half of the 20th century with Julian, Bogan, Curie, and Kennedy. The advent of charter schools in the late 1990s and early 2000s yet saw another expansion of the league as schools such as CICS, Noble Street, ACT Charter and Northside Prep were included. The CPL as it stands today is very diverse with nearly every major nationality and race represented in all sports.

ADMINISTRATION

The CPL is head by the Director of Sports Administration and Facilities of the Chicago Public Schools. As of the start of the 2007-08 school year, Calvin Davis holds this position since taking over for Dr. J.W. Smith in 2003. Under the Director are Sports Coordinators, who govern competition in the sports that they are assigned. Some coordinators handle multiple sports; one example is Mickey Pruitt, a graduate of Robeson and a former member of the Chicago Bears. Pruitt currently governs competition in football, wrestling, and lacrosse.

BASIC PLAYING LEVELS

Nearly every sport has four playing levels; Varsity, Sophomore, Freshman and Elementary. Incoming freshman can 'play-up' to either sophomore or varsity levels; the same with sophomores for the varsity. The elementary school division was developed in the late 1990s, by Dr. J.W. Smith as a way to close the athletic gap between the CPL and its parochial counterpart, the Chicago Catholic League. Today, coaches in the high school sector and the CPL actively recruit the elementary division to fill their ranks, as opposed to earlier years where most kids came into the high school athletic arena with little or no experience.

"THE SHIELD"

The championship trophy of the CPL is noted by "The Shield." It is one of the most unique sports trophies in the world. A school holding one of those trophies is recognized as having beaten a very large field of competitors for the city title. Until 2004, the trophy was made of wood with either a gold or silver plate notating champion or runner-up finish. Since 2004, it is now made of black marble with gold trimming and plated with a silver scuplture of the sport the trophy was earned in. Between 1972 and 2002, the holder of the Shield gained automatic entry into the Illinois State Finals in most sports (except football). Since then, the city championship has been decided prior to the start of the state championship.

Another reason schools play for the Shield is the venues that they play in. Every year the Shield is contested in a number of professional or major college stadiums. Over the years they have included Soldier Field, the UIC Pavilion, United Center, International Amphitheater, Chicago Coliseum, Chicago Stadium, Wrigley Field, Comiskey Park - US Cellular Field, Loyola University, Chicago State University, Northeastern Illinois University and DePaul University.

ATHLETIC DIVISIONS

With the exception of football, girls basketball and baseball, each sport in the CPL has two distinct playing divisions; Red and Blue. The Red Division is considered the highest level of competition city-wide, while the Blue features programs just starting or not quite as talented. In football, there are three divisions; the Illini (Red) Conference, the Chicago (Blue) Conference and the Intra-City (Green) Conference. In baseball, various divisions are notated by the names of famous major league baseball players, with the highest competition division being the Jackie Robinson conference. In girls basketball, there are three divisions; Red, Blue and Green.

BASKETBALL

CPL sanctioning of basketball dates back to 1913, when the CPL was formed. The CPL didn't play for a state championship until the 1926-27 school year, when it first joined the IHSA. The basketball ranks have enjoyed the most success at the state tournament of any sport sanctioned by CPS. The first state title for the CPL basketball came in 1958 with Marshall, some four years after DuSable earned the league's first ever state championship berth. Including that championchip, CPL schools have enjoyed the top of the podium 27 times, 17 of those on the boys side. Eight of the ten girls titles also belong to Marshall, thanks to the state's all-time winningest coach in the sport, Dorothy Gaters, who at last count had 881 wins for he career.

Among the stadiums used to stage the city championship were the Chicago Coliseum, International Amphitheater, the UIC Pavilion, and recently the United Center. When the boys championship was contested for the time at the United Center in 2000, the league set a new state attendance record in basketball as 20,002 patrons watched Westinghouse earn the crown against Whitney Young. To date, every championship game that was held at the United Center earned more fans than the present state championship sites of Carver Arena in Peoria and Redbird Arena in Bloomington combined.

The most city basketball championships for boys is a dead heat as Crane and Marshall each have 11 Shields. There's no question who is the top team in the girls ranks, Marshall, with 23 championships - the most by a single sports team (boys or girls) in league history. Nevertheless, basketball in the city is still extremely competitive as girls teams have been gaining on Marshall, especially Whitney Young.

The 2007-08 season North Lawndale competed in the Public League Red North-West and in Class 2A in the IHSA's new four-class system. That system has opened up the possiblity of unprecedented state tournament success for the Chicago Public League, which already had two Final Four teams in the Class AA the previous two years in two-time champ Simeon and Marshall, which took third both times. Young, for instance, was ranked No.1 in the *Chicago Tribune's* preseason poll of Chicago-area teams and is joined in Class 4A by No.4 Farragut,

No.13 Curie and No.15 Von Steuben. While No.2 Simeon and No.3 Marshall are in Class 3A.

Another major change took place in April 2002, when the CPL relinquished the automatic Class AA Elite Eight berths that went to its playoff champions in several sports. While that meant that the CPL might no teams to the state quarterfinals in some sports, it did allow for the realistic possibility of more than one qualifier in basketball. Some veteran Chicago Public League coaches feared giving up the automatic berth would mean years in which no CPL team would reach the Elite Eight, but at least one team has made it every year since the change. In 2004, 2006, 2007 and 2008, at least two teams made it.

It has been five decades since that breakthrough game, and the most surprising thing now is that Chicago high school basketball ever had to break through anything. Its success, at first elusive and then a surprise, has long since been almost an assumption, and it's easy to see why. Since March 22, 1958, when Marshall won Chicago's first state basketball title, Chicago Public League schools have won 16 more crowns and 15 runner-up or third -place trophies.

In 2008, two Public League teams met for a state championship for the first time in Illinois state basketball history. Marshall defeated Simeon to win the Class 3A boys basketball title. Chicago North Lawndale won the Class 2A title while representing the Public League. Two weeks prior, girls titles at Illinois State University was won by Marshall in Class 3A and Whitney Young in Class 4A.

Marshall became only the second team in Illinois history to win both the boys and girls state basketball championship in the same season. The only other team to win both titles in the same year was Teutopolis. In the Commandoes' 69-61 Class 3A championship win over Simeon, the first-team Associated Press all-stater Ryan Hare, led Marshall with 19 points, six rebounds and five assists. While, Simeon got a monster performance from 6-foot-9 inch Illinois signee Stanley Simpson, who finished with 28 points, nine rebounds and six blocks.

CHICAGO PUBLIC LEAGUE BOYS BASKETBALL CHAMPIONS

COOK COUNTY HIGH SCHOOL LEAGUE (1901-13)

YEAR	CHAMPION	RUNNER-UP	SCORE
1901	Hyde Park	North Division	23-22 (ot)
1902	Medill	Lake	16-15
1903	North Division	Medill	41-14
1904	North Division	Austin	26-19
1905	Austin	Lake	62-22
1906	Oak Park	Austin	21-14
1907	Lake View	Austin	24-21
1908	Lake View	Austin	25-21
1909	Lake View	Calumet	(a)
1910	Englewood	Calumet	30-18
1911	Lane	Hyde Park	34-29

| 1912 | Hyde Park | Lyons | 19-18 |
| 1913 | Hyde Park | Englewood | 11-9 |

CHICAGO PUBLIC HIGH SCHOOL LEAGUE (1914-PRESENT)

YEAR	CHAMPION	RUNNER-UP	SCORE
1914	Parker	Lane	18-16
1915	Lane	Calumet	23-7 (b)
1916	Hyde Park	Marshall	24-20
1917	Phillips	Lane	22-11
1918	Englewood	McKinley	21-8
1919	Schurz	Englewood	17-12
1920	Lane		
	Hyde Park		
1921	Crane	Hyde Park	21-8
1922	Austin	Lane	27-9
1923	Tilden	Hyde Park	(d)
1924	Lane	Phillips	18-4
1925	Hyde Park	Lake View	17-11
1926	Lane	Englewood	31-17
1927 (e)	Englewood	Lane	20-17
1928	Crane	Englewood	20-19
1929	Crane	Lindblom	23-17
1930	Phillips	Morgan Park	20-19
1931 (f)	Crane	Phillips	30-22
1932	Crane	Calumet	25-21
1933 (g)	Lake View	Bowen	25-17
1934 (h)	Lane	Tilden	29-16
1935	Tilden	Senn	33-24
1936 (i)	Farragut	Kelvyn Park	23-21
1937 (j)	Wells	Farragut	23-21
1938	Von Steuben	Hyde Park	27-24
1939	Lane	Hirsch	30-25
1940	Crane	Hirsch	35-23
1941 (k)	Manley	Marshall	38-34
1942	Lindblom	Kelly	41-25
1943	Kelvyn Park	Lindblom	28-26 (ot)
1944	South Shore	Harper	51-37
1945	Senn	Von Steuben	57-32
1946	Tilden	Marshall	54-49
1947	South Shore	Lane	58-38
1948	Marshall	Von Steuben	57-32
1949	Tilden	Marshall	54-49
1950	Tilden	Vocational	45-35
1951	Parker	Von Steuben	64-58

13

1952		Roosevelt	Tilden	63-62
1953		DuSable	Wells	82-74
1954		DuSable	Lake View	82-65
1955		Marshall	Crane	67-57
1956		Dunbar	Hyde Park	79-68
1957		Crane	Marshall	66-61
1958		Marshall	Dunbar	68-59
1959		Marshall	Crane	61-58
1960		Marshall	Crane	79-38
1961	(l)	Marshall	DuSable	64-61
1962		Carver	Marshall	47-39
1963		Carver	Harlan	57-51
1964		Crane	Dunbar	63-58
1965		Marshall	DuSable	69-55
1966	(m)	Marshall	Dunbar	81-68
1967		Harlan	DuSable	60-56
1968		Crane	Marshall	75-65
1969		Hirsch	Bowen	72-66
1970		Harlan	DuSable	72-63
1971		Harlan	Tilden	44-38
1972		Crane	Marshall	75-63
1973		Hirsch	Parker	55-53
1974		Morgan Park	Phillips	84-73
1975		Phillips	Morgan Park	65-60
1976		Morgan Park	Vocational	75-60
1977		Phillips	Westinghouse	77-65
1978		Westinghouse	Manley	71-68
1979		Manley	Westinghouse	88-83 (2ot)
1980		Manley	Collins	67-56
1981		Westinghouse	Marshall	79-66
1982		Marshall	Crane	58-48
1983		Marshall	Collins	67-62
1984		Simeon	Robeson	44-42
1985		Simeon	Carver	65-54
1986		King	Simeon	67-57
1987		King	Crane	93-66
1988		Simeon	King	66-59
1989		King	Simeon	67-57
1990		King	Westinghouse	83-48
1991		Marshall	Westinghouse	58-38
1992		Westinghouse	King	76-68
1993		King	Westinghouse	77-52
1994		Westinghouse	King	59-58
1995		Farragut	Carver	71-62
1996		Westinghouse	Farragut	55-46

1997	Young	Manley	72-50
1998	Young	King	67-46
1999	King	Westinghouse	59-39
2000	Westinghouse	Young	82-60
2001	Morgan Park	Crane	67-60
2002	Westinghouse	Farragut	62-58

Notes

(a) Lake View finished 1st in 4-team division A round robin playoff; Calumet finished 1st in division A and won game with winner of division B for rights to 2nd place.

(b) No regular season games played; playoffs only

(c) Tied in title game; noovertime played

(d) Tilden finished 3-0 in round robin playoff; Hyde Park finished 2-1. Tilden beat Hyde Park 30-11, on March 10.

(e) Beginning in 1927, Public League teams began joining the IHSA and playing in the state tournament.

(f) Harrison finished third in the state tournament, despite an 0-3 record in the North-West Division playoffs.

(g) Lake View qualified for state tournament.

(h) Lane and Marshall qualified for state tournament.

(i) New Phillips (later named DuSable) qualified for state tournament.

(j) Beginning in 1937, the Public League champion received an automatic berth in the state finals.

(k) The Public League did not send a representative to the state tournament in1941.

(l) Public League divided into Red and Blue Divisions.

(m) Only Red Division teams eligible for conference title and state tournament

(n) All teams again eligible for conference title and state tournament.

(o) Beginning in 2003, the Public League champion no longer received an automatic berth in the finals.

Chicago Catholic League

The Chicago Catholic League (CCL) is a high school athletic conference in Chicago, Illinois. The schools are all part of the Illinois High School Association. The conference is made up of the male teams from the member schools and it also has a sister conference, the Girls Catholic Athletic Conference (GCAC).

History

The Chicago Catholic League was formed in 1912 as a way to give the all-male Catholic schools of the area interscholastic competition. Most of the schools that formed the league are still around today and have enjoyed great athletic and academic success. Some of the charter schools that remain as of the end of the 2006-07 school year include Chicago Mt. Carmel, St. Rita of Cascia, Leo, De La Salle, St. Ignatius and Loyola. Prior to 1974, when the Illinois state football playoffs began, other schools that participated in the league but have since left include Chicago Holy Trinity, Chicago St. George, Chicago St. Phillips, and DePaul Academy. Also, Archbishop Mendel was a long time member of the CCL until a name change in the 1990s turned it into St. Martin de Porres; that campus is now under Chicago Public League auspices as Gwendolyn Brooks Prep. Archbishop Weber was also a long time member of the CCL until shutting down for good before the 1998 high school football season.

The move to form the league was precipitated when the dominant high school league in the metropolitan area, the Cook County High School League, rejected the application of the two Catholic high schools. Early in the fall of 1912 St. Ignatius Academy and DePaul Academy applied to join the Cook County League, and found that their applications were subject to a "delay." The Catholic schools could smell a whiff of anti-Catholicism in the league's rejection, and a movement began in early October to form a football league. They gathered eight schools for the groundbreaking meeting - DePaul Academy, St. Ignatius Academy, St. Rita's College, St. Cyril's College, Cathedral High, St. Phillips High, Loyola Academy, and De La Salle Institute, but could not get together on the particulars of the league.

Finally, in the third week of November, the schools managed to form a league and drew up a schedule of games in basketball and indoor baseball. The founding members of the league were St. Stanislaus, De La Salle, DePaul, St. Ignatius, St. Cyril, St. Phillips, and Cathedral. Loyola Academy did not initially join. By the spring when a baseball schedule was drawn up, Holy Trinity and Loyola had joined the league, but Cathedral dropped out, leaving an eight-team circuit. In the fall of 1913, the league introduced football. More schools joined the circuit before the decade was up, St. Patrick in 1913, and St. Mel in 1918.

Because the Catholic school population relative to the mainstream public secondary schools and the private schools was more an immigrant and working class population, the sports that the league initially sponsored reflected this demographic makeup. For example, during the first four years of the league's existence, only baseball, basketball, indoor baseball, and football were offered. Basketball was the most robust sport, as the league not only provided for heavyweight and lightweight schedules, but also bantamweight (added in 1919) and flyweight competition (added in the early 1920s). The Chicago Public High School League and Suburban League offered basketball only in the heavyweight and lightweight classes, after experimenting only a few years with a bantamweight class. The Catholic League added track and field in 1917, but it was not until 1924 that three "country club" sports were added to the league's schedule; golf, tennis, and swimming. The addition of these sports brought the league up to the level of offerings by the Chicago and Suburban public leagues, which helped raise in the Catholic minds anyway that they were fully American, and fully worthy of being treated as equals. The 1920s also saw the addition of more schools to the league; St. George, Joliet De la Salle, and Fenwick.

MEMBER SCHOOLS

- St. Ignatius College Prep
- De La Salle Institute
- Mount Carmel High School (Chicago)
- St. Rita of Cascia High School
- Loyola Academy
- Leo Catholic High School
- Fenwick High School
- Brother Rice High School
- Gordon Technical High School
- Hales Franciscan
- Providence Catholic High School
- Guerin College Prep (Holy Cross and Mother Guerin, two single sex schools combined to form)
- Bishop McNamara High School
- St. Francis De Sales
- Seton Academy
- St. Laurence High School
- (Defunct) Weber High School
- (Defunct) St. Martin de Porres Academy

BASKETBALL

Hales Franciscan, Leo, Mount Carmel, and Fenwick (girls) have won state championships. Brother Rice recently earned a berth in the Elite Eight (2005) and St. Laurence, De La Salle and Loyola have advanced as far as the final 16 in the state tournament in recent years. The conference is divided into a North and a South Conference. The border schools in the conferences flip conferences every two years. Recently the league has instituted a 'crossover weekend', where teams in their corresponding places battle each other for bragging rights, with divisional leaders vying for the league crown in February prior to the state tournament.

NOTABLE BASKETBALL ALUMNI

- Lloyd Walton, Mount Carmel - Marqutte University, former NBA player
- Mel McCants, Mount Carmel - Purdue University, former NBA player
- Mike Krzyzewski "Coach K", Weber - Duke University basketball coach
- Antoine Walker, Mount Carmel - NCAA Champion Kentucky Wildcats in 1996, NBA Champion Miami Heat in 2006 starting forward
- Corey Maggette, Fenwick - NBA basketball player

- Andre Brown, Leo - DePaul University, NBA basketball player

BASKETBALL

Recently the Catholic League has been dominated by Brother Rice, Leo, Loyola, Hales Franciscan, and Fenwick.

STATE CHAMPIONS

- 2005 - Hales Franciscan - Class A
- 2004 - Leo - Class A
- 2003 - Hales Franciscan - Class A
- 1985 - Mount Carmel - Class AA
- 1979 - Providence Catholic - Class A

STATE RUNNER-UP

- 1993 - Hales Franciscan - Class A
- 1990 - Gordon Tech - Class AA
- 1988 - St. Francis de Sales - Class AA
- 1982 - Mendel Catholic - Class AA

CHAPTER THREE

SOUTHERN ILLINOIS CONFERENCE OF COLORED HIGH SCHOOLS

Sometimes basketball can be more than just a game. Basketball can also be a way of life invariably under certain circumstances. When the East St. Louis Lincoln Tigers hoisted the trophy the night of March 20, 1982, it was their first state championship. There may have been more exciting title games than Lincoln's 56-50 victory over Chicago Mendel Catholic, but few were more significant. Staking a claim to the Tigers' trophy were neighboring Brooklyn Lovejoy and 13 other schools once barred from state tournament play; the members of the former Southern Illinois Conference of Colored High Schools (SICCHS).

African-American players and teams had already etched their names into state-finals lore. Peoria's Lynch Conway, the tournament's first great black athlete, scored 22 points in the 1908 championship game. Chicago New Phillips sent the first all-black squad to the state in 1936. Meanwhile, relegated to a league of their own, was the SICCHS - 15 schools located in three geographic pockets essentially south and west of a line running from St. Louis through Benton to Paducah, Kentucky.

Near St. Louis in the Metro-East counties of Madison and St. Clair were five schools; Brooklyn Lovejoy, Edwardsville Lincoln, East St. Louis Lincoln, Madison Dunbar, and Venice Lincoln. The second cluster of schools was four in number, squeezed into a small square in the middle of "Egypt," the 17 southern most counties of Illinois; DuQuoin Lincoln, Colp, Murphysboro Douglas, and Carbondale Attucks. The Deep South or Ohio River schools were located near Kentucky in the two southern tips of the state. Four of them; Cairo Sumner, Mound City Lovejoy, Mounds Douglas, and Sandusky Young were located near Interstate 57. The two others - Brooklyn Lincoln and Metropolis Dunbar were located near Interstate 24.

Southern Illinois shared much with the American South in both geography and tradition. The three areas of the SICCHS represented the lingering segregation in Illinois prep basketball. Racial segregation was a resolute way of life in the southern third of Illinois. As a result, some of the finest coaches, players, and teams the state has ever seen were unjustly isolated from the rest of Illinois.

Organized around 1919 and segregated from their neighbors as well as other IHSAA members, SICCHS schools were forced to maintain a low profile. The first barrier fell in 1929 when the ISHAA (as it was known until 1940) allowed the SICCHS schools to join the association. Membership did not include all the privileges, however. The IHSAA provided trophies for the conference's annual postseason tournament, but little more in the way of assistance.

After more than a decade of admitting the SICCHS schools, the state association took the first steps toward making them equal partners. Starting in 1942, the IHSA organized two district basketball tournaments for the conference, with the winners meeting in Huff Gym during the state finals. From 1942 to 1945, this "Colored Conference championship game" played at the state tournament was wedged between Friday's quarterfinal session.

The evolution of integration in southern Illinois required many difficult decades, but the process would have been even longer and grueling had it not been for high school basketball. In fact, it was the game of basketball, possibly more than any other single factor, that helped break segregation's stronghold in southern Illinois. In addition to slow but steady advances by the IHSA, some schools on the northern fringes of the southern third of the state began to strike blows for integration. Two all-white schools were the most courageous in the quest to eradicate segregation from high school basketball in the region.

On Christmas Eve 1945, Livingston High School hosted an all-black squad from Madison Dunbar in the first integrated basketball game played in the southern third of the state During Christmas week one year later, Gillespie High School became the first all-white team from southern Illinos to play a basketball game on the court of an all-black school as its team traveled to Madison Dunbar. Not to be overlooked was the courageous contribution of Dunber, which stepped across convention and beyond age-old cultural lines to play all-white schools.

In 1946, the IHSA Board of Directors voted to allow SICCHS shools into the state tournament. Winners from the all-black district tournaments advanced to regional tournaments as close as a host school would accept them. That usually meant somewhere near the northern fringe of what was called "Egypt." Mounds Douglas refused by two regional tournaments, finally gained acceptance at Benton, where Floyd Smith, president of the IHSA, was principal.

On February 28, in the regional semifinals, Douglas upset second-ranked West Frankfort 55-51, sending shock waves throughout the state. The celebration was short-lived, however. The next night, Johnston City buried Douglas 59-38. Douglas and Carbondale Attucks dominated the Deep South district from 1946 to 1953, although Cairo Sumner won the honors once, in 1948. Meanwhile, in the Metro-East, Madison Dunbar and East St. Louis Lincoln took turns winning district championships.

The winners, however, had trouble competing with larger schools in regional action. It was 1949 before a SICCHS school finally won a regional tournament. East St. Louis Lincoln accomplished the feat, but lost to the Brownstown Bombers in the sectional semifinals.Madison Dunbar followed suit the next season losing a first round sectional game to Collinsville. in 1952, Carbondale Attucks met No.2 Centralia in the sectional final at West Frankfort, taking the Orphans to the wire before surrendering a late lead and losing 71-64. Finally, following the 1952-53 season, basketball segregation officially vanished from the south as illinois completely integrated its district tournaments.

In 1954, Mounds Douglass won the first integrated district tournament in southern Illinois at Anna-Jonesboro, thenclaimed the regional title at Wolf Lake, before heading to Harrisburg for arguably the toughest sectional in the state. Sparked by 6-foot-8 All-American center Archie Dees, Chicago Mt. Carmel drilled Douglass 97-68. Three years later, East St. Louis Lincoln became the first SICCHS school to crack the AP statewide poll, compiling a 28-0 record and climbing to No.11 in the rankings. However, that Tigers team, fueled by a standout player named Bennie Lewis, slipped in the regional final against crosstown rival East St. Louis Senior.

In addition to Mounds Douglass, only three other SICCHS teams won regional tournaments after 1953. East St. Louis Lincoln finally broke through in 1958, and both Douglass and Carbondale Attucks duplicated the feat in 1960. In the 1960 semifinals, Metropolis ousted Attucks 66-60 in overtime, while Douglass took West Frankfort to a pair of extra sessions before losing 71-69.

East St. Louis Lincoln became the first former SICCHS school to win a sectional tournament reaching the 1980 Carbondale Super-Sectional only to lose against Effingham and 7-foot-2 Uwe Blab 74-58. Two years later, in 1982 Lincoln went a near-perfect 29-1, beating Chicago Mendel to capture the school's first state title. It was also the first state championship for a former SICCHS school, the culmination of a generations-long dream. By the decade's end, the Tigers would add three more championships in 1987, 1988, and 1989. Lincoln merged with East St. Louis Senior following the 1999 season, leaving only Brooklyn Lovejoy as a surviving SICCHS school. The rest eventually consolidated with other schools. Lincoln has the highest tournament winning percentage (.800) of any school with at least five tournament visits.

CHAPTER FOUR

GREAT DOWNSTATE BASKETBALL HIGH SCHOOLS

CENTRALIA HIGH SCHOOL

Centralia is located in Marion, Jefferson, Washington and Clinton Counties in Illinois. The population was 14,136 at the 200 census. The town was founded because it was the point where the two original branches of the Illinois Central Railroad, built in 1856, converged. The town is named for the railroad.

On March 25, 1947, the Centralia No.5 coal mine explosion near the town killed 111 people. The Mine Safety and Health Administration of the U.S. Department of Labor reported the explosion was caused when an underburdened shot or blown-out shot ignited coal dust. At the time of the explosion 142 men were in the mine. Sixty five men were killed by burns and injuries and forty five by afterdamp. Eight men were rescued but one died from the effects of afterdamp. This is slightly ironic as a more famous Centralia, Pennsylvania is best known for being the site of a mine fire.

Over the course of its 150-year history, Centralia, Ill., has weathered more than its share of setbacks. The Illnois Central Railroad traffic that put the town on the map has long since disappeared. Coal mining virtually stopped overnight following the 1947 mine disaster that killed 111 miners. The oil boom, which at one time made the surrounding countryside resemble a derrick factory showroom dried up in the 1950s. But through good times and bad, Centralia has managed to hold onto a constant source of community pride and pleasure. For nearly 70 years, the Centralia Orphans have been the "winningest" high school boys basketball team in the United States. With a lifetime record of 1,937 wins and 814 losses at the close of the 2002-2003 season, the Orphans have celebrated more victories than any other boys' high school basketball team in the country.

The high school was orignally located of the site of the current Centralia Community College, and torn down in the late 60's and was relocated to 813 Eshoom Road. Its famous basketball alumni include; coach Arthur L. Trout, Dwight "Dike" Eddleman, Bobby Joe Mason and Dick "Eldo" Garrett. Until recent years, Arthur Trout was the winningest coach in Illnois history with 809 career victories. He has also won three state championships (1918, 1922, 1942). Dike Eddleman is generally acknowledged as the greatest male athlete in state history. Bobby Joe Mason played 15 seasons with the Harlem Globetrotters. While, Dickie Garrett made the NBA All-Rookie team playing for the Los Angeles Lakers.

After Trout retired in 1950, Jimmy Evers produced some outstanding teams in the 1950s (he was 105-22 from 1951 to 1955), and Bill Davies coached 29-2 and 29-3 teams in 1961 and 1962. Rich Rapp, an All-Stater on the 1961 team, said the old-timers still insist that the best game ever played was Collinsville's 66-64 victory over Centralia in the 1961 supersection in Salem. But as long as the game is played in Centralia, they will remember 1963 team, the 32-2 powerhouse that was top-ranked in the state but lost in the state final to Chicago Carver 53-52 on Anthony Smedley's dramatic last-second steal and game-winning shot.

TAYLORVILLE HIGH SCHOOL

The IHSA single season Boy's Basketball record of 45-0 was set by Taylorville High School in 1944. Ron Bontemps and Johnny Orr were team members on that team. Bontemps would later become the captain of the 1952 U.S. men's basketball team, which won the gold medal. He played in all eight matches in the 1952 Summer Olympics. Johnny Orr became the winningest coach in Iowa State University men's basketball history. He also coached the Univesity of Michigan to national runner-up in the 1976 NCAA Championship.

Taylorville is a city in central Illinois, incorporated in 1882. The town of around 12,00 residents (15,000 plus people in the greater-Taylorville area) is located twenty-five miles southeast of Springfield, the capital of Illinois, and twenty-three southwest of Decatur. Their Tornadoes under coach Dolph Stanley, became the first unbeaten boys basketball state champion in the history of the state tournament. In the 1940s and 1950s, the gym which was built in 1938 there was always filled to capacity.

In 1942-43, Taylorville was ranked number one in the state at the end of the regular season. But they finished 29-2, losing to Decatur, with Eddie Root and Glenn Jackson, 39 36 in the sectional. However, the tradition turned into legend in 1943-44 when Taylorville went 45-0. The top-ranked Tornadoes beat beat third-ranked Champaign four times, the last time 40-36 in the state semifinals. Stanley had scheduled several state powers that season. They beat Pinckneyville by eleven when both teams were unbeaten. They also beat second-ranked Canton, Paris, Centralia and Mount Vernon.

The team didn't really lose much luster after Bontemps and Orr graduated and Stanley left in 1946. In 1950 and 1952, Taylorville reached the state quarterfinals with 5'7" guard Bill Ridley. However, Stanley's Tornadoes were the biggest thing ever to hit Taylorville, an old coal-mining , farming, and railroad town southeast of Springfield. In the 1944 state finals, they trounced East St. Louis 52-34 and Kewanee 51-30, got past Champaign by four, then smashed Elgin 56-33 for the championship. Orr scored sixty four points in the four games; Bontemps had forty nine. Both were named to the all-tournament team.

PINCKNEYVILLE COMMUNITY HIGH SCHOOL

Pinckneyville is the county seat of Perry County, Illinois. The population was 5,464 at the 2000 census. Pinckneyville is approximately 70 miles southeast of St. Louis, Missouri and 300 miles southwest of Chicago. It lies about 30 miles to the east of the Mississippi River. Growth boomed in the 1850s for two reasons: construction of the Illinois Central Railroad, and the discovery of large coal reserves. Mining continued to be the dominant employment sector through the 1990s, when Clean Air Act regulations devastated the Illinois coal economy.

The Pinckneyville Community High School is known for its basketball, winning State Championships in the sport in 1948, 1994, and 2001. Merrill "Duster" Thomas and Dick Corn are two legendary coaches from Pinckneyville. Merrill Thomas arrived at Pinckneyville in 1935. Thomas put Pinckneyville, a coal-mining town, on the map. Pinckneyville annually battled two other celebrated programs, Centralia and Mount Vernon for bragging rights in southern Illinois. He was big on fundamentals, discipline, and meetings. The 1946-47 team was 32-7 and finished third in the state. However, the 1947-48 Panthers won thirty-three of thirty-four games. The Panthers lost to Edwardsville in the final of the Mount Vernon Holiday Tournament.

In the sectional final in 1948, they beat Centralia by one. Their toughest matchup came against Pekin in the state semifinal, whom they had beaten in the 1947 state consolation game. Pekin was ranked number one in the state. Pinckneyville beat them 36-31. In the final, the overwhelmed Rockford East 65-39 to win the state title. Afterwards, townspeople bought Thomas a new car, a 1949 Packard. They later named the new gym after him. Built in 1952, with a seating for about twenty-five hundred, it remains one of the best high school facilities in the state. After it opened, the team won fifty-eight games straight at home. Thomas retired in 1957 after winning 495 games.

Dick Corn was hired in 1975. His first two teams got to the sectionals, his third team struggled to .500, but his fourth team was 29-4. They won its first conference title in fifteen years, and lost in the supersectionals. For thirteen seasons straight, from 1983 to 1996, Corn's team won twenty or more games. He has won more than six hundred games, including state championships in 1994 and 2001, and a runner-up trophy in 1988.

Mount Vernon High School

Centralia was the winningest high school in the nation. Coach Arthur Trout and three-time All-Stater Dike Eddleman were legendary figures in southern Illinois. But within ten years, coach Stan Changnon had escaped from Centralia's shadow by achieving a milestone that Centralia has never surpassed thus far. Mount Vernon has won four state titles, whereas Centralia has won only three.

In 1949, Mount Vernon was ranked number four in the state, but lost its last regular season game to Johnston City by one. After winning the sectional to earn a trip to the Sweet Sixteen, they beat Johnston City in the first round by two, then swept Decatur 71-51, West Aurora, and Hillsboro to win the state title. With Max Hooper, Riley and King returning in 1949-50, the Rams were a popular choice to repeat.

As expected in 1949-50, the Mount Vernon Rams were dominant. One of their closest games was a 57-48 victory over Elgin in the state semifinals. In the final, the Rams crushed second-ranked Danville 85-61 as Max Hooper scored thirty -six points, setting a then state tournament record for points scored in the final. They outscored Danville 45-28 in the second half to pull-away for their second consecutive state title.

Moore and Riley returned in 1950-51, and Mount Vernon was ranked sixth in the state. The Rams forty-six game winning srteak was snapped by Centralia, and they lost to Pinckneyville in the sectional. Picnkneyville's coach Duster Thomas is credited with devising a brilliant plan to upset Mose Stokes, who fouled out early in the game.

In 1951-52, Mark Mannen, Joe Johnson, Don McCann, and Mose and Jim Stokes led Mount Vernon to third place in the state tournament. The Rams were 32-4, losing to Quincy 54-51 in the semifinals, then beating Rock Island 71-70 in the consolation game. It was Changnon's last season. He retired to become the athletic diretor.

In 1953, Mount Vernon lost a one-pointer to Harrisburg in the sectional final as Al Avant missed the last shot. He may never have forgotten the experience, but with four starters returning, there was high expectations for the 1953-54 season. Harold Hutchins, a pupil of Changnon's , was in his second season, but Changnon still ran the program, sometimes coming onto the gym floor to direct practice. They were 20-3 and ranked fourth in the state after the regular season. They split a pair of games with Don Ohl and Edwardsville, which finished fourth in the state. They were well balanced, with all five starters averaging in double figures; Avant (sixteen ppg), Goff Thompson (thirteen), Don Richards (fourteen), 6'5" center Larry Whitlock (fifteen), and Fred Deichman (ten).

In the sectional, Avant converted two free throws after time had expired to beat Chicago Mount Carmel and Archie Dees by one. Afterwards, they would beat Danville in the first round of the Sweet Sixteen. Later, they trounced Moline in the quarterfinal, and Pinckneyville in the semifinals. Thus, setting the stage for a unbelieveable state final against Chicago DuSable, the talk of the tournament. Coach Jim Brown's DuSable Panthers were undefeated.

Chicago DuSable sported three all-staters; Paxton Lumpkin, Shellie McMillon and "Sweet" Charlie Brown. After the Panthers had smashed Chicago Bowen, Quincy, and Edwardsville in their first three state tournament games, everyone outside of Mount Vernon predicited a rout in the championship game. But the game was tied after three quarters. Then Mount Vernon, with Avant scoring twenty-three points and Richards twenty-five, pulled away to win 76-70. However, there was considerable controversy over the officiating, especially after a charging foul sent Lumpkin out of the due to fouls, and two walking calls against Brown in the closing minutes.

Nevertheless, later on coaches Gene Haile, Bob Arnold, Lee Emery, and Doug Creel would take the Rams back to the state finals. There were more good players too; including Coleman Carrodine, Terry Gamber, Nate Hawthorne, Jamar Sanders, and Kent Williams. However, the glory of the 1950s has to be duplicated. Mount Vernon didn't send another team to the Elite Eight from 1969 to 1997. In 1997, Kent Williams and company lost to West Aurora in the quarterfinals. In his three seasons at Mount Vernon, the Rams were 25-5, 25-4, and 28-1. He also finished as the school's all-time leading scorer with 2,185 points, but still would lose to East St. Louis and Darius Miles in the 199 supersectional.

COLLINSVILLE HIGH SCHOOL

Once a coal-mining center, the city now has food-products and clothing industries. Collinsville is located mainly in Madison County, and partially in St. Clair County, both in Illinois. At the 2000 census, the city had a population of 24,707. Collinsville is approximately 12 miles due east from St. Louis, Missouri and is considered part of that city's metropolitan area. Famously, it is the home of the world's largest ketchup bottle (a 170 foot tall water tower in the shape of a ketchup bottle), and is the self-proclaimed world horseradish capital. The city and surrounding area are said to produce 85% of the world's horseradish, of such high quality that it's actually exported to Germany and China (key users of the herb) for gourmet use.

Collinsville High school, the Kahoks, named for a fictional Native American tribe, have won several Illinois State Championships. In 1961 and 1965, they won state championships in boys basketball.Former coach Vergil Fletcher, who was named one of the 100 "Legends of Illinois high school basketball" by the IHSA won over 700 games in his career. Other famed Kahoks were Kevin Stallings, now Men's Head basketball coach of Vanderbilt University; Bogie Redmon, also a "top 100 legend," who played on the undefeated 1961 team; Tom Parker, a star at the University of Kentucky after his Collinsville high school days; and Richard Keene, a McDonald's All-American, who played at the University of Illinois in the 1990s.

Basketball was king at Collinsville even before Vergil Fletcher became a legendary coach, and taking fourteen teams to the Sweet Sixteen and winning two state championships. Collinsville had already established a winning tradition. In 1937, Willard Larson's 27-4 team finished third in the state. in 1946, the year before Fletcher arrived, Jack Fabri's 30-10 team reached the state quarterfinal.

Collinsville expected to win its first state title in 1956-57. Led by a pair of All-Staters, 6'7" Terry Bethel and 6'5" Thom Jackson, the Kahoks won their their first 34 games and were ranked number one in the state. Bethel was named to *Parade* magazine's All-American team, but in the state final against Herrin, which had lost to Collinsville at Centralia in December, Bethel picked up three quick fouls in the first five minutes of the game and was forced to sit down. Collinsville shot only seventeen of forty seven from the field and Herrin won 45-42.

Collinsville went 32-0 in 1960-61. Bogie Redmon and Fred Riddle were returning starters from the 1959-60 powerhouse team that was ranked second in the state before losing to Granite City in the regional at Collinsville. Although Redmon and Riddle were all-staters, Bob Simpson's steal in the closing seconds to key a 66-64 victory over second-ranked Centralia helped save the Kahoks' seasons that year. Next, the Kahoks crushed their last three opponents that had reached the Elite Eight by margins of twenty-three, thirty-seven, and thirty-four points to become acclaimed one of the top five teams in state history. Redmon scored niety-two points in four games and Riddle scored seventy-six to finish first and second amongst tournament scorers

After two-time All-Stater Roger Bohnenstiehl failed to reach the state finals in Champaign in 1963 and in 1964, (his 26-3 and 28-1 teams lost to Centralia in the supersectional at Salem) coach Fletcher turned in arguably his best coaching job of his career in 1964-65. The team had no one taller than 6'3" center Dennis Pace. Not even Fletcher expected to win the state title, however, they were ranked number eight in the stat after the regular season.

Pace would make fourteen of his first fifteen shots taken, including eleven of twelve in the first half, as Collinsville crushed Lawrenceville 82-58 in the supersectional. The Kahoks smashed Lockport 70-45 in the quarterfinals, then beat Chicago Marshall and Rich Bradshaw 76-64 in the semifinals. In the final, they held of Quincy's late rally to win 55-52. Current coach Bob Bone, who played on Fletcher's teams in 1970-73, still coaches the ball-press, and implements Fletcher's old rules in what is now, Vergil Fletcher's Gymnasium.

EAST ST. LOUIS LINCOLN

East St. Louis is a city located in St. Clair County, Illinois on the Mississippi River opposite St. Louis. It was incorporated in 1859. As of the 2000 census, the city had a total population of 31,542. One of the highlights of the city's waterfront is the Gateway Geyser, the tallest fountain in the United States, which spews water to a height of 630 feet and is designed to mirror the Gateway Arch across the river in St. Louis. Once a rail and transportation hub with stockyards and warehouses, East St. Louis has suffered serious econmic decline; in 1994 Illinois took over operation of the city government. Oil refining, steel, chemicals, glass, and construction materials have all been important industries, but unemployment, population loss, and social problems have wracked the city since the 1960s. A riverboat gambling casino is now a major employer.

The first settlement here was in 1765. Cahokia Creek was bridged in 1795, and a ferry across the Mississippi began operation shortly thereafter. East St. Loius was plagued by devastating floods until its first dike was completed in 1909. Several destructive tornadoes have hit East St. Louis, the deadliest being the St. Louis-East St. Louis Tornado of 1896 which killed at least 255, injured over 1,000, and incurred an estimated $2.9 billion in damages (197 USD).

In 1982, a decade of dominance in Illinois boys high school basketball for East St. Louis and coach Bennie Lewis began. The first of four state championships in an eight-year period came with a 56-50 win over Chicago Mendel Catholic. Elite Eight scoring leader Michael Hampton got seventh-ranked Mendel into the title game with a 22-footer as the clock ran out on top-ranked Quincy. In the bellam, nobody could've heard the horn if it had gone off, so when Quincy's coach Jerry Leggett claimed the buzzer had to sound, he was given a timeout. The buzzer did eventually sound with the scoreboard reading Mendel 53, Quincy 52. But by comparison, the title game seemed tame as Todd Porter paced East St. Louis Lincoln (29-1) with 22 points in the final victory of the tournament.

In 1987, East St. Louis Lincoln was not the state finals focus at it zeroed in on the first of what would be a record three straight championships. However, unbeaten Quincy stunned unbeaten and top-ranked Peoria Manual in the quarterfinals by making its last 13 shots from the field, including a pull-up 26-footer by 5-foot-6 guard James Bailey with two seconds left in overtime for a 61-59 victory. With Manual no longer in the fold, third-ranked East St. Louis took over.

The Tigers, led by 6-9 junior LaPhonso Ellis, pounded Chicago King 79-62 in the title game for the first title of their triple crown. Ellis turned in a thunderous performance with 27 points and 10 rebounds, and 6-8 James Harris added 23 to the count, but those players didn't dominate the game. Instead it was 6-8 Mr. Illinois Basketball Marcus Liberty, registering a Class AA record 41 title game points and 15 rebounds for Chicago King who got that honor. Freshman teammate Jamie Brandon, a future Mr. Illinois Basketball, added 12 points for King in defeat.

Marcus Liberty, who would be named national prep player of the year, ended with a Class AA Sweet Sixteen record of 143 points for a 34.0 ppg average. Brandon would end his prep career in 1990 with 3,157 points, the most by any player to reach the Class AA Elite Eight. His career 269 points that came in Sweet Sixteen play was also a record for the state tournament. Quincy would up placing fourth, maiking coach Jerry Leggett the first coach in state tournament history with a complete set of Class AA final four trophies. Manual's Dick Van Scyoc joined that exclusive club with a win in the 1994 title game, as would St. Joseph's Gene Pingatore with his 1990 championship.

In 1988, East St. Louis Lincoln's 6-10 LaPhonso Ellis got 26 points and 15 rebounds, while his 6-9 Chicago St. Francis de Sales counterpart Eric Anderson got 23 points and 17 rebounds in the title game. But Lincoln won the war 60-52 with the help of 20 points and 10 rebounds by junior Cuonzo Martin. This duo of Ellis and Martin made the middle season the strongest of the Tigers' record setting three consecutive title years. Ellis averaged 25 point in this Elite Eight and Martin scored at a 17-point pace.

Ellis set the Class AA Sweet Sixteen career rebounding record with 82 rebounds in six games. A year later, Martin would up the record to 87, a total that he established in nine games. Peoria Manual's Sergio McClain set a new standard of 101 by 1997, but he would play in the Sweet Sixteen four consecutive years. Anderson and Ellis wound up one-two for Mr. Illnois Basketball, respectively.

In 1989, not only did the Tigers complete the state's first triple crown, they did it in a triple overtime. Many considered that season's title game to be the most marvelously contested title game in Illinois state history. With one second left in triple-overtime, Vincent Jackson's 18-footer under double-team pressure at the top of the key gave Illinois' Jewel of the Mississippi (29-4) and coach Bennie Lewis a 59-57 vivtory over second-ranked Peoria Central. And, thus the state's consecutive title record in the process. Cuonzo Martin led Lincoln with 20 points. While, Mike Hughes (21) and Charles White (20) paced Central.

PEORIA MANUAL

Peoria is the seat of Peoria County, Illinois and is the center of an urban complex consisting of Peoria Heights, West Peoria, Bartonville, Bellevue, East Peoria, Creve Coeur, and Pekin. The city is considered the oldest continuously inhabited American community west of the Allegheny Mountains. Peoria is located in northwest-central Illinois, north of Springfield. It was incorporated as a town in 1835, as a city in 1845, and is the largest city on the Illinois River. As of the 2000 census, the city had a total population of 112,936. It is a transportation and industrial center.

Peoria has become famous as a representation of the average American city because of its demographics and its perceived mainstream of Midwestern culture. The city's general makeup is almost identical to that of the United States as a whole, thus making it an ideal test market for consumer researchers. On the Vaudeville circuit, it was said that if an act would succed in Peoria, it would work anywhere. The question "Will it play in Peoria?" has become a metaphor for whether something appeals to the American mainstream public.

In 1994, Peoria Manual won the first of an incredible four straight state championship in boys' basketball by beating Carbondale 61-60. Down by one with a couple of seconds left on the clock, senior guard Brandon Hughes converted a one-and-one free throw situation with the title on the line. Ironically, both teams were improbable trophy winners by drawing the two top-ranked Elite Eight entries in the quarterfinals. The third-place game was even more surprising matching a pair of unranked teams, LaGrange Lyons and Rockford Boylan.

LaGrange, in a game that marked the end of coach Ron Nikcevich's 33-year coaching career at 562-288, beat Boylan 56-42 for third. But while the titile game was story book ending to the prep career of Hughes, the season proved to be the final chapter in the legendary saga of Manual coach Dick Van Scyoc. The season left the 45-year head coach (28 at Manual) with his first state championship and an 826-400 record that included the all-time state record for boys' prep coaching victories, surpassing the legendary Arthur Trout, who went 809-344 at Centralia from 1914 t0 1951.

In 1994-95, coach Van Scyoc left Peoria Manual to successor Wayne McClain. Wayne McClain, who had played for the state's all-time boys' win leader when Van Scyoc led the Rams to fourth in 1972, was poised for the job. In the regular season, McClain and Manual went 10-1 against teams ranked in the top 16 at least sometime during the season, beating the number ones of Illinois (Chicago Farragut) and Missouri (St. Louis Vashon).

Second-ramked Manual was but one of four top-16 entries in the Peoria Sectional, including Peoria Central and all-stater A.J. Guyton, who would eventually be a Big Ten MVP at Indiana. Then Manual needed to beat its historical nemesis, No.14 Quincy, to reach Champaign for an Elite Eight also packed with the No.1, 3, 5, 7 and 8 ranked teams in the state. In the quarterfinal in Champaign they defeated Hersey 64-36, and in the semifinals they were victorious over third-ranked Joliet Township 62-60.

Coach Rocky Hill and Harvey Thornton defeated Chicago Farragut and its two Mr. Basketballs (6'11" Kevin Garnett this season, high-flyer Ronnie Fields the next) 42-39 in the quarterfinals. Thornton was considered a team with more athletes than Manual. They would met in a final that featured the first modern state-title of first-year head coaches. Manual defeated Thornton 65-53 to win its second consecutive state title. The 1995 Class AA tournament was the last played in Champaign-Urbana after a run of 77 years. Manual got 20-point games from senior all-state guards Willie Coleman (also a title-game record seven steals) and Ivan Watson. All-around Thornton athlete Tai Streets moved on to a football career in the Big Ten and NFL, and sophomore teammate Antawn Randle El would soon follow a similar path.

In 1996, the state finals moved into the Rams backyard, the Carver Arena court in the Peoria Civic Center. Manual had survived the Peoria Sectional by beating a fourth-ranked East Peoria team, and it took a last-second 24-footer by sophomore Frank Williams to do it. Next, second-ranked Manual got double-digit scoring from all five starters to stop a talented sixth-ranked Springfield Lanphier team in the Normal Supersectional. After defeating Hinsdale Central in the quarterfinals, they poised themselves for a third consecutive state title.

Harvey Thornton had rolled past third-ranked Rock Island 51-34 in the quarterfinals. In the semifinals the Wildcats cruised past Chicago Westinghouse 69-54 to reach the finals a second consecutive time. Manual defeated Thornton 57-51 for the state title in the Class AA tournament's title-game rematch. It was also the first Class AA title game to match teams ranked No.1 and 2 in the final regular season poll. With the victory, Manual (31-2), tied East St. Louis Lincoln's 1987-89 record run of three consecutive Class AA titles.

Fro two years straight, 6'10" Melvin Ely and Thornton had everything it took to win a state championship. But the Wildcats wasn't able to get it done against the Rams big men, and guard Frank Williams who led all scorers with 17 on 7-for-10 shooting. A reserve might have actually made the difference though. Manual's 6-foot Marshall Dunnigan had only a half-dozen points and rebounds, but he always seemed to be at the right place at the right time. Tragically, six weeks later, the well-regarded student-athlete and son of a veteran Peoria policeman was murdered. He was unfortunately the random shooting victim of a gang member on Peoria's south side.

In 1997, three-time defending champ Peoria Manual and two-time runner-up Harvey Thornton would up on the same side of the tournament bracket. It made for a spirited semifinal with Manual beating Thornton 65-62. It took three years, but the Associated Press state pollsters had finally learned, ranking once-beaten Manual on top, and unbeaten Thornton second in the final regular-season poll. The unlock of the draw kept the Rams and Wildcats from competing in a third straight state final. However, nothing kept them from ending one-two in the national *USA Today* rankings.

Thornton didn't even catch it's breath until they outscored Rockford Boylan by 21 points in the second half to win the third-place game. But some Wildcats keep right on going; center Melvin Ely to Fresno State and the No.12 overall

NBA draft pick, forward Napolean Harris to Nortwestern and the NFL, and guard Antawn Randle El to Big Ten football MVP and a Super Bowl ring. While Sergio McClain (the coaches son) and teammate Marcus Grifftih would end up one-two in Mr. Basketball voting and would move on to Big Ten titles at Illinois. Frank Williams was named Mr. Basketball the next year, and eventually became a Big Ten MVP at Illinois. In a seemingly anti-climatic title game, Sergio McClain led all title-game scorers with 22 in a 47-43 victory over West Aurora. Sergio also ended his prep career having started every post-season game for four years and going 32-0 as Manual became the first Illinois high school team to win a state-title four consecutive years. Whereas, Thornton had only four losses in three years, but three of them was to Manual on the last day of three straight seasons.

LAWRENCEVILLE HIGH SCHOOL

Lawrenceville is a city in Lawrence County, Illinois, along the Embarras River. The population was 4,745 at the 2000 census. It is the county seat of Lawrence County. Lawrenceville is located in southeast Illinois, about 10 miles northwest of Vincennes, Indiana. The city is home to an old Texaco oil refinery that is now a Superfund site. Lawrenceville has only one radio station, WAKO AM and FM. It has a somewhat comical history. The original owner, Stuart K. Lankford, lost the radio station and other holdings during a poker game with other notable community leaders, notably Tyler Howard, mayor during that time.

The city is home of the Lawrenceville Indians, Illinois Class A high school state basketball champions in 1972, 1974, and back-to-back in 1982 and 1983, which had a combined two season win-loss record of 68-0. Those teams were coached by Ron Feeling, who after the 1983 season at Lawrenceville, went on to Indiana as assistant to Bobby Knight. At Lawrenceville, Feeling also won 83 percent (388-77) of his games, and produced such outstanding players as Marty Simmons, Jay and Dennis Shidler, Doug Novsek, Rick Leighty, and David Brooks.

In 1972, Lawrenceville won the first Class A state championship with the largest enrollment (630 students) in the Elite Eight. The Indians started the season 5-6, but led by 6-foot-3 sophomore forward Rick Leighty won the first of four state titles under coach Ron Feeling. The historic first Class A title-game was an all-south match-up against Meridian before a crowd of 11,554 at the University of Illinois Assembly Hall. Lawrenceville benefited from the best game of senior guard Mike Lockhard's career. While his teammates struggled, Lockhard exploded for 32 points on 15-for-28 shooting to fuel a 63-57 victory.

As he had two years earlier, Rick Leighty stepped up when his team needed him most. A senior who was all-tournament during Lawrenceville's first title run, Leighty was honored again after scoring 24 points and grabbing 11 rebounds in a 54-53 championship win over Ottawa Marquette. Of Leighty's 18 second-half points, the most significant came on a pair of free throws with 3:06 left that gave Lawrenceville (30-3) a three-point lead. After the tournament, Lawrenceville retired Leighty's No.34.

During the 1975-76 season, guard Jay Shidler scored ,1013 points, avaraging 32.7 points per game, as Lawrenceville won twenty-nine of thirty-one games and finished third in the Class A tournament. He set a state finals record with 157 points in four games, including forty-eight in a semifinal loss to Oneida ROVA and forty-five in a consolation victory over Buda Western. More than 14,300 showed up for the third-place game against a Buda Western team that had lost only once in thirty-two games. Shidler's record stood for twenty-five years, until Westmont's Pierre Pierce scored 159 in 2001.

The Lawrenceville Indians were the first Class A champions and in the first decade of Class A basketball provided some of the most memorable small-school tournament moments. So it seemed fitting when, in 1982, Lawrenceville (34-0) became the first Class A champion to finish the season undefeated. Perfection didn't come without its share of difficulties either. Top-ranked Lawrenceville had to battle with teams in the Elite Eight that owned a combined record of 231-24, a .906 winning percentage that ranked the best in Class A history. All-staters Doug Novsek and Marty Simmons both made the all-tournament team. Novsek was the tournament's scoring leader with 94 points in four games.

The 1982-83 team was led by Simmons, a 6-5, 230 pounder who was Illinois' Mr. Basketball, and was the number five scorer (2,986 points) in state history. He scored 1,087, an average of 31.9 per game. The team averaged seventy-nine points, while its opponents scored only fifty-two. Lawrenceville had its toughest test in the state quarterfinals against a Chicago Providence-St. Mel team that would win the Class A title in 1985. The Indians broke out to a 16-4 lead, but St. Mel rallied behind Lowell Hamilton and Michael Parker. Lawrenceville won 56-54, as Simmons scored all of his team's twenty-three points in the second half.

In the title game against Flanagan, Marty Simmons was held 12 points under his season average but still led Lawrenceville with 20. Flanagan's 7-foot center Bill Braksick had 19 points and eight rebounds, but his running mates would score only eight field goals and four free throws. Lawrenceville's 44-39 win put Ron Feeling in the record books as the first coach to win four state titles. Lawrenceville's fourth state championship also tied the record held by Mt. Vernon.

CHAPTER FIVE

GREAT CHICAGO-AREA BASKETBALL HIGH SCHOOLS

DuSABLE HIGH SCHOOL

DuSable High School is a Bronzeville high school located on the South Side of Chicago that opened in 1934. It was named after Chicago's first non-native inhabitant and trader, Jean Baptiste Pointe du Sable. DuSable was first built to accomadate the growing Phillips High School in the 1930s, but instead was renamed. It is one of the most famous schools in Chicago.

DuSable High was surrounded by the Robert Taylor Homes, a predominantly black housing project, once the largest in the U.S., though now almost completely demolished. The school primarily serves students from tthe Homes and the Bronzeville area, explaining DuSable's current 99% black student enrollment. A number of famous alumnus attended school there including Nat "King" Cole, Harold Washington, Redd Foxx, Gene Ammons, Ronnie Boykine, Don Cornelius, Kevin Porter, and Maurice Cheeks. Dr. Margaret Taylor-Burroughs, a prominent artist and writer and co-founder with her husband of the DuSable Museum of African-American History, taught at the school 23 years.

The DuSable Panthers of 1954 was the first all-black team with a black coach to reach the highest levels of an organized integrated, tradition sports program in America, when it gained the finals of the state tournament in Illinois. However, the title game could've been seen as a confrontation between big city and rural town, between black and white, and between north and south since Illinois was sort of divided that way. Paxton Lumpkin was the captain of the team in his senior year.

As a junior he was a star with the DuSable team that won the city championship, under a white coach, and then went to the state tournament where the Panthers would lose in the first round to eventual tournament winner, LaGrange Lyons. Lumpkin was the high scorer in that game with 29 points. Now he and two other standouts from the team, Shelli McMillon and "Sweet" Charlie Brown had been joined by McKinley Cowsen and Karl Dennis to roundout the first five. Lumpkin, McMillon, and Brown savored a return to the state tournament as seniors. They were three of the best players in the state and were supremely confident of their skills, especially Lumpkin. The nucleus of the team, Brown, Lumpkin and McMillon had been playing together all year round for nearly four years now, and they could almost sense where the others were on a basketball court.

Coach Jim Brown was respected and admired by the players as well as the community for the work he did with the basketball team. He was thirty-six years old in 1954, and had a sense of humor as well as sense of the dramatic. The season before, Brown had been an assistant basketball coach to white head coach, Art Scher, a small, gray-haired fifty-four-year-old white man. However, Scher could not command the powerful control over the players that Brown, younger and black, could. Brown became the head coach after Scher received a transfer to Sullivan High School. Scher lived in an apartment close to Sullivan, which was located in a white neighborhood.

The 1953-54 Panthers' team averaged over eighty points per game at a time when averaging seventy was virtually unheard of. They scored over 100 points in a quarter of their games. Another stunning statistic was that they averaged 95 shots at the basket in these high school games that lasted only thirty-two minutes. One the other hand, the Panthers' defense was a glaring defect, particularly when opponents broke their full-court press. The Panthers' would gamble a lot on steals of the opposition's passing or dribbling. Many of DuSable's gambles resulted in easy rival baskets. Nevertheless, in the last regular season game the Panthers beat Tilden for its twenty -fourth in a row over the regular season.

DuSable opened the city playoff, one-game elimination contests involving sixteen teams, with two easy wins. In the city semifinals a good McKinley High team, with Clarence Wordlaw scoring twelve of his twenty-six points in third period, gave DuSable trouble. But the Panthers characteristically pulled away in the end for their twenty-seventh straight victory. Next, they met Lakeview to determine the city representative in the Illinois High School state tournament downstate. The game was played in one of the finest gyms in the city, Weber, a Catholic school and a neutral site. The Panthers captured their second consecutive City League basketball title with a 82-65 victory

The state tournament, as was the city playoffs, a single-game elimination of sixteen teams. The games were played in Huff Gymnasium on the University of Illinois. It was a four-day tournament with the semifinals and finals being played on the same day. The Chicago teams had been considered the joke of the state tournament. In the forty-six previous years of state tournament play, up to 1954, no Chicago team had ever made the finals. Only one, South Shore in 1941, had made the semifinals. However, in this tournament DuSable and Pinckneyville were considered the favorites, according to sportswriters. Each was listed as 3-1 odds in the sixteen team field. Molin was only 5-1, Quincy and Mount Vernon were 6-1, and Edwardsville 7-1.

Up first for DuSable was Bowen Township High School, a team that won thirty of its first thirty-two games. Huff Gymnasium was filled to the capacity of 6,913. The score was 49-49 with one minute left in the third quarter. They went on to outscore Bowen 31-15 in the final quarter, and won 87-64. DuSable next met Quincy at 7:30 on Friday night. Near the end of the third quarter it was DuSable 48, Quincy 47. But DuSable sprinted out in front again in the fourth quarter and trampled Quincy, 80-66.

On Saturday afternoon, DuSable steadily outscored Edwardsville until at one point their led was twenty points in the fourth quarter. DuSable's pace was furious and the also contained Edwardsville's star, Don Ohl, a 6-2 guard with a jump shot that tournament observers believed could only be matched by Sweet Charlie Brown. Against DuSable, Ohl only scored nine points while the Panthers' Lumpkin scored thirty-one. Mount Vernon upset Pinckneyville, 70-44. They both were neighboring southern Illinois towns with an intense rivalry.

The Mount Vernon Rams had not lost a title game in three previous tries, while the Panthers had not won a championship in two previous trips to Champaign. The championship game was a classic. In one of the most controversial games in tournament history, the Panthers drew even at 70 late in the fourth quarter, but fouls and turnovers kept them off the board down the stretch. Before it was over, three DuSable players had fouled out, Lumpkin and Brown in the last 11 seconds. Mount Vernon shocked previously unbeaten DuSable 76-70. The memorable upset made Mount Vernon the state's first four-time titleist.

MARSHALL HIGH SCHOOL

Marshall High School is located on Chicago's West Side. Throughout the years, their boys' basketball program has been one of the best in the city. The stories within the story made the 1958 IHSA Boys' Basketball Tournament special. The first was the exceptional play of Chicago Marshall sophomore sensation George Wilson, a 6-foot-6 defensive wizard and inside scoring threat. Against Elgin in the Evanston super-sectional, Wilson held the Maroons' 6 11 center George Cook scoreless on only four shots in a 63-43 romp. Wilson also led the state tournament with an average of 21.5 points per game.

Yet, another story centered on Marshall, undefeated in 27 games and vying for the Windy City's first state championship. The final story was the appearance of the top-ranked teams in the title game. Rock Falls, ranked No.1 all season long, and Marshall, ranked first in the postseason polls after pronosticators tossed Marshall into the mix. Those two teams entered the championship clash with a combined won-lost record of 63-1.

Marshall had assumed the favorite's role after an impressive showing against third-ranked Herrin in the quarterfinals. The 28-3 Tigers and defending state champs kept losing ground, finally failing in its quest for a repeat title, 72-59. In the title game Rock Falls grabbed the early led and carried a 53-52 led into the stretch run. But Marshall took control late and captured an exciting 70-64 win, the Commando's 31st win in an umblemished season. The first state champions from the city of Chicago, The Marshall team returned home to a heroes welcome in the loop.

In 1960, Chicago Marshall returned to Champaign with a vengeance. State champs in 1958, first-round victims in 1959, the Commandoes were 27-2 with a trio of returning starters; 6-foot-8 all-American center George Wilson, and frontline teammates Ed Franklin and Ken Moses. Charles Jones and sparkplug Eddie Jakes, along with sixth man Jim Pitts, filled out the most physically intimidating squad in the 53-year history of the state finals. Thirteenth-ranked Elgin was the first to fall on Marshall's relentless march to the title game, losing 71-55 in Evanston. Monmouth was next, losing by 20 points in the quarterfinals. Only seventh-ranked

Stephen Decatur stayed relatively close to the Commandos, falling 74-62 in Saturday's first semifinal.

Both Marshall and Bridgeport benefited from some early giant-killing as four ranked teams stumbled in the super-sectionals, and three more fell in the quarterfinals. That left only two survivors from the AP poll standing. In the final match-up, Marshall overpowered the much smaller Bulldogs. Bridgeport didn't have a chance. Hounded by the Commandos' size and speed, the Bulldogs shot only 32 percent from the field, and their defense was unable to stop Marshall's inside-outside scoring punch also.

The Chicagoans stormed out to a roaring 28-18 lead after one quarter. The score was 44-30 at half-time, and an unsurmountable 63-39 after three quarters. All five Marshall starters scored in double figures as the Commandos won easily 79-55. Marshall annexed their second title in three years. In a four year period from 1957 through 1961, Marshall won thirty-one, twenty-five, thirty-one, and twenty-eight games, and lost eleven, claimed two state championships, a third-place finish, and lost a one-pointer in the supersectional. George Wilson became an icon in the city joining Thornton's Lou Boudreau and Centralia's Dike Eddleman as one of few three-time All-Staters in Illinois history.

CARVER HIGH SCHOOL

Carver High School is located on the South Side of Chicago. Many of the students that attended there grew up in Altgeld Gardens, a self-contained housing project near the school on Chicago's far South Side. Chicago Carver, which had not even fielded a basketball team until 1956, was unranked at 25-4 at the start of the 1962 postseason. Still, they were poised for a run at the IHSA boys' basketball title, with an attack featuring 6-5 all-American guard Cazzie Russell and 6-6 junior center Joe Allen, one of the most intimidating players in the state.

In the first round of the state tournament in Champaign, Carver overcame a Chicago St. Patrick defense that held Russell to only eight points, hanging on for a 48-42 win. Carver next upset top-ranked Centralia, 56-50, as Russell and Allen scored 22 and 16 points, respectively, while the Challengers' defense limited the Orphans to 29 percent shooting. Carver had an easier time against little McLeansboro, running past the Foxes 54-41, as Russell poured in 25 points.

Carver opened the championship game, against the Runnin' Reds of Stephen Decatur, with an 11-2 stretch. The referee disallowed another Carver basket when he blew his whistle in response to a time-out request from the Chicago team's bench. Shortly afterwards, Allen tumbled to the floor with a knee injury and left the game, never to return. But Carver still led 20-10 after one quarter.

With Allen out, the Reds moved move freely on offense while Carver lost its inside game. Decatur still trailed, but only 27-25 at half-time. They would seize the led, and after three quarters was up 39-43. Carver rallied at the close of the game, tying the score. Then, with less than a minute to play, The Challengers' Bruce Raickett, who earlier had taken a blow to the head, passed the ball directly to Decatur's Jerry Hill. The Reds waited for the final shot. Ken Barnes, a 6-foot-3 all-state senior was fouled with six seconds to play. His first free throw provided the winning margin. Despite Russell's game-high totals of 25 points and 15 rebounds, Carver fell agonizingly short of the coveted crown. Decatur captured its fourth state title in thrilling fashion, 49-48

In the 1963 state finals, Huff Gym, with its sell-out crowds of 6,925, gave way after 37 years to the spacious and sparkling-new Assembly Hall, where a record 16,310 fans watched Saturday's semifinals. No.1 Centralia at 31-1 and three unranked teams started the day in quest for the state title. It became one of the most memorable Saturday's in tournament history.

Peoria Central held a tenuous 19-17 halftime lead, but was dead-even with Chicago Carver when 6-6 center Joe Allen made a layup to force an extra session. Carver won in overtime 40-37. What followed was a timeless North-South showdown. Carver's 15-12 first quarter lead grew to 21-14 before Centralia surged to close the gap. The score was 30-26 at the half, 43-39 after three quarters, and 47-41 when the Orphans rallied. Centralia was in front, 49-47, with less than three minutes left to play.

Kevin Maxey's four free throws, the last with 2:10 remaining, gave Carver a 51-49 lead. Centralia's Rich Zgol's free throw trimmed the margin to one, and when Herb Williams hit a jumper with just 30 remaining, Centralia recaptured the lead, 52-51. Twelve seconds later Allen's pass into the paint was batted away and picked up by Centrali's Williams. He dribbled twice and then handed the ball to teammate, Don Duncan. Duncan then called an ill-advised timeout. Carver's coach Larry Hawkins inserted a defensive specialist, sophomore guard Anthony Smedley.

Duncan inbounded the ball to Williams, who was promptly double-teamed. After a controversial no-call, Williams attempted a quick pass. Smedley batted the ball and then stole it, pivoted once, dribbled to the baseline, and launched a hurried 18-footer. That was only his third shot attempt of the tournament, but it went in putting Carver back in front 53-52. As the horn sounded, Robert Cifax partially blocked a desperation jumper by Centralia's Cliff Berger, giving the city of Chicago its third state title in six years. Centralia, who produced standout players Dike Eddleman, Bobby Joe Mason, and Dick "Eldo" Garrett, is still haunted by those memories.

PROVISO EAST HIGH SCHOOL

Proviso East High School serves the educational needs of four villages within the Proviso Township, namely Maywood where it is located, Broadview, Forest Park and Melrose Park. Maywood has an ideal central location 10 miles west of downtown Chicago. The population was 26,987 at the 2000 census. There are many spacious century-old homes in relatively unaltered condition, and Maywood boasts 16 homes and properties listed on the National Register of Historic Places. Maywood and the rest of Proviso Township has a rich history.

Prior to being split into East and West, East was known as Proviso Township High School. Proviso East is a comprehensive four-year high school.

Since the fall of 1911, Proviso East has been graduating students. Proviso East graduates who have reached the NBA include; Sherrell Ford, Doc Rivers, Jim Brewer. Michael Finley, Dee Brown, Steven Hunter, Shannon Brown, and Donnie Boyce.

In 1969, the Proviso East Pirates became the first top-ranked team to win a state championship in eight years, and Proviso East coach, Tom Millikin joined Freeport's Glenn "Pat" Holmes as the only men to play on and later coach state championship teams. While Holmes did it at Freeport, Millikin was a member of "Duster" Thomas's 1948 title team at Pinckeyville. Coach Millikin had a premier post player in 6-foot-6 all-American Jim Brewer and an exceptional cast. Top to bottom they were the best team in the state.

The semifinal showdown between Champaign and Proviso East was one of the most memorable games in years. Down 36-35, Proviso East stalled away the games final seconds, spreading its offense for Brewer to go one-on-one against all-state center Clyde Turner. Making his move, Brewer popped a 17-foot jumper. Fouled on the play, his two free-throws with only 6 seconds remaining, won it 37-36.

After that the title game was almost anti-climatic. Proviso East took command early, sweeping to a 28-15 lead at the break, and coasted to a 58-51 victory. Peoria Spalding was the first private school to have reached the championship game. The 1969 state championship was the first of four so far for Proviso East, which also won titles in 1974, 1991 and 1992.

In 1974, Proviso East (29-4) methodically banged the boards with such leaders as 6-5 all-state center Jon Ponsetto to win the title 61-56 over Bloom and Audie Mathews. Mathews, rated the nation's No.2 prep player behind Moses Malone, had a nightmare of a final, missing 17 of 23 shots for the third-ranked Trojans. Bloom led at the start of the fourth quarter but was outscored 21-13 in the final eight minutes. The late Coach Glenn Whittenberg (301-68) had left the south (Herrin) to follow fellow southern Illinois native Tom Millikin to where the talent was, in this case Proviso East. Wittenberg's drill-instructor style was best evidenced by the way his hair was cut, a flat-top in an era when some teams looked like a bunch of rock stars.

In 1991, the Pirates toughest pressure might've been the great expectations from having a team with three all-staters. The closest state finals call for the Pirates, however, was a three-point semifinal win over Libertyville, which lost by two to Marshall in the third-place game. Libertyville still took what was then only the second boys basketball trophy in Lake County history (Waukegan was fourth in 1952). Top-ranked Proviso East faced fifth-ranked Peoria Manual in the title game.

Peoria Manual had 5-foot-10 point guard Howard Nathan, by five inches the shortest Mr. Illinois Basketball honoree in the first 22 years. Proviso East had three future NBA players as its frontline; 6-7 Sherrell Ford, 6-5 Donnie Boyce and 6-6 Michael Finley. Both title game teams were good passing teams, but Manual had a 28-23 lead at the intermission. Then Proviso East doubled its haftime count in the third quarter, and the Pirates won its third championship 68-61.

In the end, Proviso East was where it was predicted to have been, while No.2 West Aurora, and No.3 Chicago King failed to reach the Sweet Sixteen.Finley would later become only the second IHSA product in nearly a century of state tournaments with both a prep championship and NBA all-star recogniton. The other champ and all-star was Dike Eddleman of Centralia's 1942 state championship team.

In 1992, Coach Bill Hitt enjoyed his second consecutive state championship. He called it a victory for the program, as three Proviso East head coaches had hand in four titles over 22 years. This came under the watchful eye of Tom Milliken, the only person to be a player (Pinckneyville '48), coach (Proviso East '69), and principal (Proviso East '74) at state title schools. The only unbeaten team coming into the state tournament left with an unblemished record when top-ranked Proviso East defeated seventh-ranked Peoria Richwoods 42-31. It was the lowest scoring state championship game since Dike Eddleman suited up for Centralia halfa century earlier.

Lyons (LaGrange) Township High School

Lyons Township High School in LaGrange, originally founded in 1888, is now called North Campus and is used by Juniors and Seniors. Freshmen and Sophomores go to the South Campus, founded In 1956, located In neighboring Western Springs. The Campus was split due to lack of available land for expansion around the original building. Previously there was a junior college associated with the high school but due to increasing enrollment, lack of space, and new rules that separated junior colleges from high schools, it was merged with College of DuPage in 1967.

LaGrange is a suburb of Chicago in Cook County. The population was 15,608 at the 2000 census. The area around LaGrange was first settled in the 1830s. LaGrange's location, at approximately thirteen miles from Chicago's Loop, is not considered far at all from the city by today's standards. The BNSF Railroad runs through LaGrange. Daily commuter service on that line, connecting Aurora and Chicago is provided by Metra, and stops at two stations within the village. Amtrak also serves the station nearest LaGrange Road.

Lyons Township in LaGrange is one of three schools in state history to field two unbeaten teams. Lawrenceville (1982, 1983) and Chicago King (1990, 1993) are the others, but Lyons is the only one to prevail in a one-class playoff. When top-ranked Kankakee (26-0) met third-ranked LaGrange in the Joliet sectional of the 1953 state tournament, it lived up to its billing as the best game in the tournament . LaGrange upset the Kays 83-74 behind 6-foot-7 all-state pivot man Ted Caiazza. State scoring champion Harv Schmidt, a 6-6 center who would later play and coach at the University of Illinois, finished his dazzling career with a 37-point performance.

LaGrange opened Sweet Sixteen play in Huff Gym against up-and-coming Chicago DuSable. At the helm was coach Greg Sloan, who was in his 10th and final season at the school. All-state guard Paxton Lumpkin poured in 29 points for the Panthers, but Caiazza and the Lions were too much. Caiazza netted a game-high 31 and the favorites won handily 85-68.

Against Decatur St. Teresa the next day in the quarterfinals, Caiazza scored all of his team's 21 first quarter points, fueling a 75-43 romp. He finished with a tournament record 38 points. Pinckneyville was up next for the favorite Lyons in the semifinals. Caiazza scored 27 points, leading LaGrange to a surprisingly easy 78-65 win. The finale pitted LaGrange against Peoria Central, 29-3 and powered by 6-5 all-state center Hiles Stout. He was averaging 27 points through three tournament games.

Stout scored his average in the finale, but Caiazza countered with 25 as LaGrange claimed a 72-60 triumph and the school's first state title. LaGrange was the tournament's third undefeated champion, following Taylorville and Mt. Vernon. Caiazza ended up on top, scorching the Huff Gym nets for 121 points, shattering Max Hooper's record total of 104 from 1950. In the process, LaGrange set a four-game scoring record of 310 points, however, it stood for only 364 days.

In 1970, with Ron Nikcevich at the helm, LaGrange Lyons hoped to become the first undefeated state champion since Collinsville in 1961. Led by all-staters, 6-foot-8 junior Owen Brown, and 6-1 senior Marcus Washington, the Lions defeated all 27 opponents to become the pollsters' top-ranked team. However, in the state tournament amongst the state's top six ranked teams, only Galesburg missed making it to the Sweet Sixteen.

Lyons met unranked Effingham St. Anthony, who toppled fourth-ranked Collinsville 85-78 in double-overtime in the supersectionals, in the quarterfinals. It was an extraordinary game. At halftime Lyons seemed to be in complete control with a 50-35 lead. But St. Anthony fought back to tie the game at 77 each with 4:45 left to play. With 1:12 remaining in the game, Mike Wente's gave St. Anthony the lead at 85-84. Nevertheless, when Washington nailed a free throw with 0:02 remaining, Lyons led 89-86. Wente's uncontested lay-up at the buzzer counted but Lyons would prevail 89-88. Washington finished with twenty-eight points, thirteen rebounds, and eleven assists, a triple-double.

LaGrange defeated Joliet Central and tournament scoring leader sophomore Roger Powell 63-52 in the semifinals. East Moline upended Peoria Spalding to assure a championship game for an unranked team. Lyons held a slim 30-28 lead over East Moline at halftime in the title game. Then next, they used a 24-10 fourth quarter to bury the Panthers 71-52 as Owen Brown scored 24 points, a set a state tournament record with 24 rebounds.

KING HIGH SCHOOL

Martin Luther King Jr. High School is located on the South Side of Chicago in the heart of gang territory. The El Ruhn's headquarters was five minutes away. Fights and shootings were daily experiences for students walking to and from school. The gangs didn't bother basketball players though.

In 1986, King defeated state and national rankings leader Simeon with Mr. Basketball Nick Anderson in the supersectionals to reach the Elite Eight. King boasted 6-foot-8 all-state junior Marcus Liberty, but it was 6-6 senior Levertis Robinson who led the Jaguars past Evanston in the quarterfinals with 25 points and No.2 Peoria Manual in the semifinals with 27. It took a 10-footer with five seconds left by David Weatherall to beat unranked Evanston.

David Weatherall came back to lead all scorers with 18 points in a 47-40 title game win as King limited all-state Kendall Gill to five points on 2-of-14 shooting. The Olympians led 39-30 at halftime, but King held them to just six points in the second half. Rich Central had defeated Carbondale and all-state Steve Bardo 54-43 in the quarterfinals. Then they outscored Romeoville 73-56 in the semifinals to reach the title game.

Gill, Liberty, Bardo, Anderson, Kenny Battle (of 1984 third place West Aurora and Lowell Hamilton of 1985 Class A champion Chicago Providence-St. Mel) would all return to Assembly Hall and in 1989 spark the University of Illinois to its first NCAA Final Four in 37 years. However, the state's final would soon be known as the Terminal Three when Romeoville went from 27-6 to 0-33 and had to return the fourth-place trophy for the season-long use of an over-age Chicago transfer. Romeoville had eliminated fourth-ranked St. Joseph in the quarterfinals on a free throw with no time remaining.

In 1990, the only all-Windy City title game in state history, at that time, top-ranked King (32-0) won 65-55 over fourth-ranked Gordon Tech (30-2). It was the second Chicago title in four years for King and coach Landon "Sonny" Cox. King won with senior guard-forward Jamie Brandon getting 25 points and twelve rebounds, teammate Rashard Griffith making his title game debut as a 6-foot-11 freshman with 12 points on 6-for-6 shooting, and Johnny Selvie adding 17 points and 11 rebounds. Mr. Basketball winner Brandon ended four years of Sweet Sixteen play with a 10-3 record, and trophies for first, second, and third, a 20.7 scoring average, and an all-time tournament career record of 269 points. His all-games career total of 3,157 ranks third on the state's all-time scoring list.

After winning 30 consecutive games in the state tournament, East St. Louis Lincoln and coach Bennie Lewis settled for third place with a one-point win over Quincy in the last Sweet Sixteen for coach Jerry Leggett (528-233). King ended East St. Louis Lincoln's bid for a fourth straight championship in the semifinals with an eleven-point margin. King's coach also wound up on top when *USA Today* named Cox prep coach of the year.

In 1993, unbeaten and top-ranked Chicago King featured Mr. Basketball winner 7-0 Rashard Griffith, and senior teammate7-foot-2 Thomas Hamilton. When the smoke had cleared, the Jaguars (32-0) had Sweet Sixteen spreads of 25, 28, 31 and 37 to win going away. The latter was the widest margin of victory in any Class AA Elite Eight game, overtaking the 35-point spread in Dolton Thornridge's 1972 title win. King's average Sweet Sixteen victory margin of 30.5 points per game broke the record of Quincy '81, albeit by only a quarter of a point.

By the tournament's conclusion, King coach Landon "Sonny" Cox owned a state-record with a winning percentage of .900 for his first thirteen seasons (he ended up with a record mark of .850) and King ('90 and '93) and LaGrange ('53 and '70) were the only Class AA schools to post a pair of perfect seasons. Cox, who was fond of touting the Chicago Public League playoffs as a harder place to win than Champaign, made his own point. King would win 6 of 10 CPL finals, and in all six of those seasons the Jaguars netted at worst a third-place finish at state.

THORNRIDGE HIGH SCHOOL

Thornridge High School is located in Dolton, Illinois. Dolton is located just west of the expressway Interstate 94 and immediately south of the city limits of Chicago. Dolton is bordered by Chicago to the north; South Holland to the south, Harvey and Riverdale to the west, and Calumet City to the east. The population was 25,614 at the 2000 census. Dolton is the hometown of NFL star Donovan McNabb and *Ebert and Roeper* star Richard Roeper.

Smaller schools wanted a better chance of winning regional tournaments and earning a trip to the state finals. Subsequently, the 1971 state tournament marked the final year of single-class basketball in Illinois. In the last one-class championship game, the Thornridge Falcons was fueled by all-state guard Quinn Buckner, a junior with quick hands. Buckner and the Falcons met the unranked Oak Lawn Spartans, powered by all-state strongman C.J. Kupec, a 6-7 senoir who controlled the paint. It marked the first title game match-up between two Cook County teams in Illinois boys basketball state tournament history. Kupec and Jim Bocinsky combined for 10 points down the stretch, drawing the Spartans to 52-50 with just 30 seconds left to play. With 21 seconds left, Buckner missed a free throw. The Spartans had the last possession, but missed two shots in the final four seconds, one of which was a lay-up, to give Thornridge the win.

Perhaps no team had higher expectations than Thornridge in 1971-72. That the team would emerge as the best team in state history was largely attributed to coach Ron ferguson and team leader Quinn Buckner. Statistics set Thornridge apart from all other great teams, from Taylorville (1944) to Marshall (1958) to Collinsville (1961) to Quincy (1981) to Peoria Manual (1997). The Falcons went to win fifty-eight games in a row, a state record that stood for ten years. The Falcons averaged 87.5 ppg while permitting only fifty-three.

Coach Ferguson knew that his 1971-72 team had the makings of another championship contender. His 1970-71 team had survived in the state final, beating Oak Lawn by one-point when Jim Bocinsky's shot from the baseline bounced off the rim. However, the 1971-72 squad was better, quicker, more talented, and more experienced. To take advantage of the speed and teamwork, Ferguson devised a 1-2-1-1 zone press to disrupt opponents.

The first Class AA boys state basketball championship turned out having the same results as the last one-class championship. Thornridge forward-guard Quinn Buckner would further his image as one of the state's finest all-around athletes in state history. He also played football at Thornridge. Also, a record three Thornridge were selected all-state honorees; senior Buckner, 6-foot-7 center Boyd Batts and point guard Mike Bonczyk.

Arguably the best team in state schoolboy history, Thornridge led Quincy by 31 points at halftime of the title game and cruised to a 104-69 victory. It gave Thornridge a 33-0 season with an average point spread of 27 in its three Elite Eight games. No opponent finished closer to them than 14 points all year, prompting one coach to say that "it was almost impossible to get through Thornridge's press." They were a tenacious defensive team and all five starters could handle the ball well.

SIMEON HIGH SCHOOL

Simeon is a four-year public high school located in the Auburn Gresham neighborhood of the South Side of Chicago. Simeon was founded in 1949 as Westcott Vocational High School in a building located at 8023 S. Normal Avenue, where it operated until the Kroger company donated a vacant warehouse (located at 8235 S. Vincennes Avenue) to the Chicago Public Schools in 1963. The Chicago Public Schools renamed the school in September, 1998. Simeon operated in the Kroger building amidst horrible conditions until a new building was built, and opened for students in September, 2003.

Simeon, perhaps is well known in the Chicago area as a high school sports powerhouse, winning the IHSA Class AA State Boys Basketball Championship in 1984, 2006, and 2007. Another incident that the school is well known for is the tragic murder of Ben Wilson, a star basketball player (then widely recognized as the #1 high school basketball player in the nation) who led the Wolverines to their first state basketball championship was killed on the eve of his senior season opener (November 20, 1984). After the tragic incident, Mayor Harold Washington spoke to grieving students, denouncing gun violence in the city and promising a new gymnasium for the school, to be named in Wilson's honor. The gymnasium was completed in 1987. Today Simeon is one of the best-run public schools in Chicago.

In January 1980, after a series of disciplinary problems and charges that the basketball program was out of control, school officials offered the head varsity coaching job to Bob Hambric. At the time, Bob Hambric was supervising a biddy basketball program at Chatham YMCA. He had no intention of coaching high school basketball, but agreed to do a favor for Simeon athletic director John Everett, whose son was involved in Hambric's biddy basketball program. Hambric a no-nonsense coach, would win 528 games in twenty-three years at Simeon, one state championship, and three Chicago Public League titles. His players had to be unselfish, disciplined, and in shape.

In 1984 Chicago Simeon, the all-tall Public League champion was coming out of one bracket to contend for the state title. Despite not having a starter over 6-foot-7; Simeon's regulars averaged 6-foot-5 1/4, the fourth highest figure among Class AA champs. Ranked only No.5, Simeon completed a 4-0 season against Chicago Carver and future NBA all-star Tim Hardaway, and went 3-0 against No.7

Robeson to win the Public League playoffs. Simeon stopped perennial contender and third-ranked West Aurora and Sweet Sixteen scoring leader Kenny Battle 67-58 in the second semifinal to set up the title confrontation with Evanston, who came into the state finals with a 30-0 record.

Tim Bankston outscored Evanston all-stater Everette Stephens 25-15 in the finale to deny Evanston's bid for an unbeaten state title. The final score was 53-47. Sadly, surviving play in the Chicago Public League would take on a new and sobering meaning not only for champion Simeon but for schoolboy athletes everywhere. On the day before the next season's opening game, junior center Ben Wilson, the only non-senior starter for the 30-1 defending state champs, was shot to death near the school during lunch hour. Wilson would live in the memory of his friends at Simeon, including Nick Anderson, who wore Wilson's number (25) throughout his high school and NBA career.

In 2006, Simeon (33-4) rode athleticism, tempered by discipline to overcome the teamwork and mental toughness of Peoria Richwoods (27-7) in the state finale. Richwoods, which started 2-4 and was not among the top 20 going into the postseason, was poised for its fourth upset of this Sweet Sixteen with the ball and 15 seconds left in overtime. However, Simeon's all-state guard Derrick Rose made great plays on both ends of the court. The junior guard's steal and eight-footer with one second left gave Simeon a 31-29 victory, and Chicago its third championship in a 13-year span. The combined total of 60 points made this the lowest scoring title game in Class AA history, shoving Proviso East's 42-31 win over Richwoods in 1992 from the record books.

In 2007, The Simeon Wolverines historic win in the Class AA final marked the first time in history that a Chicago Public League team won the state championship in consecutive years, 2006 and 2007. The Wolverines didn't shy away from any challenges that season either. They faced the state's and country's stiffest competiton, defeating Oak Hill Academy, the No.1 ranked high school team in the nation, while compiling a 30-2 win/loss record. Simeon defeated Marshall 69-56 in the state semifinals, which was the first state finals meeting of Chicago Public schools. Simeon reversed a 22-point loss to No.4 Marshall with a 13-point semifinal win. They cemented their place in state tournament history and opened up future debates on who is Illinois greatest high school boys basketball team, beating O'Fallon 77-54 to win their second state title in as many years.

CHAPTER SIX

GREAT GUARDS

TIM HARDAWAY

A graduate of Carver High School on Chicago's South Side, where his was an all-state player. Point guard Tim Hardaway was one of the National Basketball Association's most exciting players for much of the 1990s. It wasn't that he was a superstar, a household name; other players placed higher in statistical rankings and grabbed headlines with slam dunks and wild antics. Yet in his prime, with the Golden State Warriors and the Miami Heat, Hardaway had speed and sheer intensity that made him, quite simply, a thrill to watch.

It was during his college days at the University of Texas at El Paso that Hardaway first developed his trademark move, a between-the-legs dribble-and-drive that was first dubbed the "UTEP Two-Step" and later the "killer crossover." Hardaway admits that he was inspired to develop the technique by Syracuse University guard Pearl Washington, whom he saw on television. Averaging 22 points per game in his senior year and returning to Chicago every summer to play in off-season leagues against NBA players, Hardaway attracted the attention of NBA scouts. He was selected in the first round of the 1989 NBA Draft by the Golden State Warriors and immediately earned a starting spot.

In the 1990-91 season Hardaway hit the level of intensity that would make him an NBA star. Hardaway was named to the Western Conference starting team for the NBA All-Star Game and ended the year with a 22.9 points per game average, touching off a string of three seasons when he scored 20 points per game. What stopped that run was a bout of knee problems that would trouble Hardaway for the rest of his career. His left knee collapsed during the Warriors' 1993 training camp, and he missed the entire 1993-94 season with a torn anterior cruciate ligament. However, after being released from his contract he ended up with the Miami Heat, and found his old intensity once again. Once again he topped 20 points per game in the 1996-97 season. Hardaway led the Heat to the NBA Eastern Conference playoff finals and was named to the All-NBA first team that year. He was named to the All-NBA second team in both 1997-98 and 1998-99.

MAURICE "MO" CHEEKS

Cheeks grew up in the Robert Taylor housing projects on Chicago's South Side and attended DuSable High School. In 1974 he enrolled at West Texas State University (now West Texas A&M University), one of the few schools that offered him a basketball scholarship. The small city of Canyon, Texas located near

Amarillo, was foreign terrain to a kid from the South Side, and Cheeks became lonely for home. During his freshman year, he became intent on leaving school and returning to Chicago. However, his mother, Marjorie, was adamant about him not quitting sachool.

At West Texas State, Cheeks was a four-year starter and three-time most valuable player on the Buffaloes basketball team. During his senior year, he averaged 16.8 points per game and shot 56.8 percent from the field. Over his entire college career, he averaged 11.8 points per game and finished fourth on the school's all-time scoring list with 1,227 points. Having played four years nestled away in a small Texas town and on a losing team in the Missouri Valley Conference, Cheeks did not have high expectations for the NBA draft. However, unbeknownst to him, he had caught the attention of Jack McMahon, a talent scout and assistant coach for the Philadelphia 76ers. During his senior year Cheeks was invited to Cincinnati to play with other NBA hopefuls in front of scouts and management. As a result of his performance, McMahon's interest spread to others in the Philly organization, and the 76ers became intent on drafting the yound point guard. Cheeks was the 14th selection in the second round, 36th overall, in the 1978 NBA Draft. For the next 11 years, he wore a 76ers uniform. He helped the 76ers earn three trips to the NBA Finals in a four-year span in the early 1980s (1980, 1982, and 1983), including one championship in 1983. In NBA history he ranks third all-time in steals and eighth all-time in assists.

Maurice Cheeks played point guard in the National Basketball Association for 15 years. During his career, the 6-foot-1 inch tall Cheeks was known for his speed, his ability to handle the ball, his consistent play, and his work ethic. Never one to seek out the spotlight, he was and continues to be admired as a person of high integrity. He was selected to NBA All-Star teams in 1983, 1986, 1987, and 1988. Overall, during his 15 year playing career, Cheeks averaged 11.1 points and 6.7 assists per game. He played in 1,101 games, scored a total of 12,195 points, and had 7,392 assists. He retired as the NBA's all-time leader in steals (since surpassed) with 2,310. One of seven 76ers who have had their number retired, his number 10 hangs from the rafters of the Wachovia Center. He's currently doing a fine job as head coach for the 76ers, and knows his role extends beyond understanding the fundamentals of basketball. He is a role model, father figure, mentor, taskmaster, and leader.

Dwyane Wade

Wade grew up in and around Chicago, Illinois and was a stand-out player at Richards High School in Oak Lawn. Wade was born in the South Side of Chicago. As a child growing up in the Chicago area Wade idolized Chicago Bulls star Michael Jordan. He did not see a lot of playing time his sophomore year at Richards as his stepbrother, Demetris McDaniel, was the star of the team. Wade grew four inches in the summer before his junior year and proceeded to average 20.7 points and 7.6 rebounds per game. Wade then averaged 27.0 points and 11.0 rebounds his senior year, and led his team to a 24-5 record. They advanced to the title game of the Class AA Eisenhower Sectional. During the season he set school records for points (676) and steals (106) in a season.

Wade played college basketball for Marquette University in Milwaukee. In Wade's first year at Marquette he did not play because of academic problems. When Wade became eligible his sophomore year (2001-2002) he led the Golden Eagles in scoring with 17.8 ppg, and also contributed averages of 6.6 rebounds per game, and 3.4 assists per game. Marquette finished with a 26-7 record, the school's best record since the 1993-94 season. In 2002-03. Wade led Marquette in scoring again with 21.5 ppg, and Marquettee won the school's first and only Conference USA championship with a 27-6 record. Wade then led the Golden Eagles to the Final Four, the school's first appearance in the Final Four since winning the 1977 national championship. After the season Wade was named to the Associated Press All-America team, becoming the first Marquette player since 1978 to do so. On February 3, 2007, nearly three and a half years after his final collegiate game, Marquette retired Wade's jersey at halftime of their game against Providence. Although Marquette requires student-athletes to graduate prior to receiving jersey retirement honors, the University made a special exception for Wade based on his accomplishments since leaving Marquette.

Selected fifth overall in the 2003 NBA Draft by the Miami Heat, Wade quickly emerged as a solid player on a relatively young Miami Heat team and averaged 16.2 points on 46.5% shooting to go along with averages of 4.0 rebounds, and 4.5 assists per game in his rookie season. Wade's successful rookie season was somewhat overshadowed by the hype surrounding fellow rookies Carmelo Anthony and, in particular, LeBron James. Wade did not disappoint in his second season. He averaged 24.1 points on 47.8 shooting, to go along with averages of 6.8 assists, 5.2 rebounds, and quickly emerged as a rising star in the league. He was selected to his first NBA All-Star Game in Denver, and came off the bench to score 14 points in the East's 125-115 win.

In the 2005-06 NBA season, Wade was selected to his second All-Star Game. In the 2006 NBA All-Star Game, Wade made the game winning put-back off of the Philadelphia 76ers' Allen Iverson's missed shot, to lead the East to a 122-120 victory over the West. He finished the 2005-06 regular season averaging 27.2 points, 6.7 rebounds, and 1.95 steals per game. Later that season, in his first trip tp the NBA Finals, in which the Miami Heat faced off against the Dallas Mavericks, Wade had some of the more well known moments of his career thus far. His performance in games three, four, and five, in which he scored 42, 36, and 43 points, respectively, helping bring the Heat back from a 0-2 deficit to lead the series at 3 games to 2. The Heat went on to win game 6, taking the series 4-2, and Wade was presented with the Finals MVP trophy. Wade had the third highest scoring average ever by a player in his first NBA Finals with 34.7 points per game.

PAXTON LUMPKIN

In a great many communities in America, the high school basketball teams represent a kind of hope, their stars holding out the possibilities of a glorious future. When Lumpkin was an all-city and all-state guard in the early 1950s, he and his team were exciting as well as inspirational to the black community in Chicago. Beyond that, it also stirred up dreams for whites, who saw the DuSable team as a symbol. The Panthers were demonstrating for everyone that when given an opportunity any underdog, by skill, drive and wit could come out from under.

Lumpkin's DuSable Panthers team would put its stamp on the sport, and there is a display about it today in the Basketball Hall of Fame in Springfield, Mass. The DuSable Panthers became the first black team with a black coach to succeed to the highest levels of integrated, organized sport in America. Along with Sweet Charlie Brown, who later starred with Elgin Baylor at Seattle University, and Shellie McMillon, who played center in the NBA for four years, Lumpkin led the team to 31 straight victories, and to the 1954 Illinois state high school championship game in Champaign against Mount Vernon, a primarily white southern Illinois team.

The DuSable Panthers played a new high school style called "run-and-gun," fast-breaking and using a full-court press. They averaged 80 points a game when other teams were still scoring 40 and 50 points. The DuSable team integrated the state tournament, and was favored to win it. But in the last 90 seconds of the game, a series of controversial calls turned the game to Mount Vernon. DuSable lost 76-70, but All-American Lumpkin was still named most valuable player in the state tournament.

Lumpkin went to Indiana University on scholarship, but books were secondary to basketball, and to dice and liquor. He flunked out after his first semester of his sophomore year. He didn't do much better at Indiana State either. After a few years with the Harlem Globetrotters, he was back in Chicago, looking for a job. In 1991, a postal worker named Paxton Lumpkin died, at age 54. He was a postal worker for several years, and he also worked with youth groups. He contracted cancer about a year prior to his death. "He was still Paxton Lumpkin, the high school star," someone from Chicago was quoted as saying.

KEVIN PORTER

A graduate of DuSable High, in Chicago, Illinois, the 6'0" point guard played 10 seasons in the NBA (1972-1981; 1982-83). Porter played collegiately at Saint Francis University, in Pennsylvania. He was a member of the Baltimore/Capital/Washington Bullets, the Detroit Pistons, and the New Jersey Nets. Porter was one of the most talented passers in league history, leading the league in both assists per game and in total assists four times during his career (1975, 1978, 1979, and 1981). At one point, Porter held the record for most assists in a game, with 29. (Scott Skiles broke the record when he tallied 30 assists on December 30, 1990.)

Porter was also a key member of the 1975 Bullets team which reached the NBA Finals before losing to the Golden State Warriors. When he retired in 1983, he had accumulated 5,314 career assists and 7,645 career points. Following his retirement from the NBA, Porter reinforced the Toyota Super Corollas Basketball Team in the Philippine Basketball association and played for one conference. He's back in Chicago working with youth groups at the James Jordan Boys and Girls Club on the cities West Side.

MICHAEL FINLEY

Finley attended Proviso East High School in Maywood, Illinois, graduating in 1991. In Finley's senior season, Proviso East won the 1991 IHSA Class AA boys basketball tournament, and Finley was named to the all-tournament team. Finley's teammates included future NBA draftees Sherrell Ford and Donnie Boyce.

The 6'7" shooting guard/small forward was originally drafted out of the University of Wisconsin by the Phoenix Suns as the 21st overall pick of the 1995 NBA Draft. Finley held the all-time scoring record at Wisconsin for eleven years, but was passed by Alando Tucker on March 10, 2007. At Wisconsin, his nicknamed was 'shooter.'

He had an impressive rookie season, being named to the 1995-96 NBA All-Rookie First Team, finishing third in Rookie of the Year voting after averaging fifteen points, 4.6 rebounds and 3.5 assists per game. He became only the third rookie in Suns history to score over 1,000 points in a season. Despite his solid play, he was traded to the Dallas Mavericks on December 26, 1996 by the Suns.

In his first season with the Mavericks, he led the team in scoring, assists and steals Along with another former Sun Steve Nash and forward Dirk Nowitzki, he became an integral part of the Mavericks "run-and-gun" offense in no time. The trio was often called "The Big Three." He was selected to represent the Western Conference in the 2000 All-Star Game, in which he scored 11 points. In 2001 he was again selected to represent the Western Conference in the NBA All-Star game. He played for the US national team in the 2002 FIBA World Championship, but the team lost a record three games, and failed to win a championship for the first time in a major competition since FIBA opened international competition to NBA players.

In 2005, Finley became an unrestricted free agent, and elected to remain in Texas with the San Antonio Spurs. In San Antonio he has adapted well to a secondary role as Manu Ginobili's backup. The Spurs were knocked out of the 2006 NBA Playoffs by his former team, one year after he made the switch. However, in 2007, Finley set the Spurs' record for three-point field goals in a playoff game, shooting 8 of 9 from beyond the arc against the Denver Nuggets. He eclipsed the previous record of 7 set by teammate Bruce Bowen in 2003. Also, Finley won an NBA championship in 2007 with the San Antonio Spurs in his 12th NBA season.

RONNIE LESTER

Though born in Mississippi, Lester grew up in Chicago, Illinois. He graduated from Dunbar Vocational High School in 1976. Lester started on the varsity team as a 5'6" sophomore. A growth spurt in between seasons rendered him virtually unrecognizable in his new 6'2" frame. He very quietly averaged ten points and ten assists per game in his junior year. As a senior, Lester had a breakout season, averaging 27 points per game. The Dunbar Mighty Men season came to an abrupt end, though, by losing to Morgan Park in the playoffs. Even though the basketball season ended on a sour note, Lester was named to All-City and All-State teams.

Basketball Hall of Fame coach Lute Olson, then of the University of Iowa, was among the first to recognize Lester's talent. At Iowa, Lester was a four-year starter, earning All-American honors in 1979, and First Team All-Big Ten honors in 1978 and 1979. He led the Iowa Hawkeyes to a share of the 1979 Big Ten title and to the Final Four of the 1980 NCAA Men's Division I Basketball Tournament. In his senior year, Lester missed 15 Big Ten games due to a knee injury. At the time he left the lineup, Iowa was undefeated and ranked among the top ten teams in the nation. He returned to the Hawkeyes lineup on March 1, 1980, for the final game of the regular season against the University of Illinois. With the consent of Illinois Head Coach Lou Henson, the Iowa Athletic Department delayed the game in order to hold a ceremony to retire Lester's jersey, and number (12). At that time, Lester already owned the Iowa records for scoring, and assists. In addition to missing 15 games, Lester's assist record was all the more remarkable given that he shared playing time with two other players ranked among Iowa's top ten in career assists.

Then, a 36 team field, with nineteen regular season wins Iowa earned a Five Seed in the East Regional of the NCAA Tournament. In the four tournament wins that it took Iowa to reach the Final Four, Lester dished out 26 assists while committing only seven turnovers. He scored Iowa's first 10 points in the semifinal game against Louisville, but after eight minutes of play reinjured his knee and exited the game. In Lester's absence, Louisville defeated Iowa by eight points and went on to win the tournament. Not counting the Louisville game, the 1980 Iowa Hawkeyes were 15-1 with, and 8-9 without him. Even after the further success and the incredible talent Lute Olson enjoyed at the University of Arizona (including four Final Four appearances, a National Championship, and players like Mike Bibby, Gilbert Arenas, and Jason Terry, Olson regards Lester as the best player he ever coached. Hall of Famer Earvin "Magic" Johnson, who played two seasons at Michigan State University, once claimed that Lester was the toughest opponent he ever faced in the Big Ten.

Lester was the 10th pick in the first round of the 1980 NBA Draft, selected by the Portland Trail Blazers. He was immediately traded to the Chicago Bulls, where he played four seasons. In 1985 and 1986 Lester was a member of the Los Angeles Lakers, winning an NBA Championship in one of two seasons. Of his seven seasons as a player in the NBA, all but two were shortened by the recurring knee injury. In his best season (1982), he averaged 12 points, three rebounds, and five assists in 75 games for the Bulls (playing with Reggie Theus, Artis Gilmore, David Greenwood, Ricky Sobers, and Orlando Woolridge). In the 1987-88 NBA season, Lester began working for the Lakers organization as a scout. As of the 2006 season, he is the Assistant General Manager of the Los Angeles Lakers.

GLENN "DOC" RIVERS

Rivers was born in Maywood, Illinois and grew up in an athletic family. Although his father, Grady, was a policeman, both his uncle Jim Brewer and his cousin Byron Irvin played in the NBA. Rivers grew up in a tough section of Chicago, but was never tempted to get into trouble because he loved to play basketball at an early age. Rivers decided that he wanted to go to a high school that had a proud basketball tradition. He had to take an entrance exam to be accepted at Proviso East High School, and he achieved the second highest test score in the school.

As a freshman, he played so well that he was called up to the varsity team for the last part of the season. During the late 1970s, Rivers acquired his nickname during a summer camp at Proviso East High School. Former Marquette coach, Rick Majerus, noticed that Rivers was wearing a Julius "Dr. J" Erving T-Shirt, and called the young player "Doc."

Rivers became a McDonald's All-American player at Proviso East, and was one of the most highly recruited players in the country. He enjoyed continued success both on the collegiate and international level. In the 1982 World Championship of Basketball, Rivers led the United States to the silver medal and was named the tournament's Most Valuable Player. After three years at Marquette University, Rivers left school early for the NBA draft. Like most athletes who leave school early, Rivers vowed to finish his education. However, he fulfilled this promise. In 1985, Rivers earned a pre-law/political science degree from Marquette.

In the 1983 NBA Draft, Rivers was selected by the Atlanta Hawks. After being selected in the second round of the draft, his first goal was to make the team. Once this was accomplished, he planned to eventually crack the starting lineup. Rivers accomplished those goals during his rookie season, and went on to become a mainstay with the Hawks. He spent eight years with the Hawks, setting team records for single-season assists (823 in 1986-87).

Following the completion of the 1990-91 season, Rivers left Atlanta to play for the Los Angeles Clippers. With Rivers in the lineup, the Clippers made a rare appearance in the playoffs. After a year with the Clippers, he moved on to the New York Knicks. The coach of the Knicks, Pat Riley, brought Rivers to New York to help stabilize the team's talented, but inexperienced backcourt. That season, Rivers led the Knicks to the best record in the Eastern Conference. The team cruised through the playoffs, and met the Chicago Bulls for the conference championship. The Knicks and the Bulls split the first four games, but New York lost the last two.

Although Rivers looked forward to leading the Knicks to an NBA championship, the rest of his career in New York was disappointing. During the middle of the 1993-94 season, he tore the anterior cruciate ligament in his left knee and was forced to sit out the rest of the season. The Knicks went on to lose to the Bulls again in the playoffs. In deceember of 1994, the knicks released Rivers. After receiving offers from six teams, he signed with the San Antonio Spurs because his main goal was to play on a championship team. The Spurs featured

David Robinson, and had brought in Dennis Rodman to help with rebounding and defense. Although the team did well during the regular season, it consistently fell short in the playoffs. At the end of the 1995-96 season, Rivers announced his retirement after 13 seasons in the NBA.

Over the course of his NBA career, Rivers averaged 10.9 points, 5.7 assists, and 3.0 rebounds per game. More importantly, Rivers was considered a solid, unselfish leader. In his 13 seasons, he led his teams to the playoffs 10 times. After the 1986-87 season, in which he averaged a double-double (12.8 points and 10.0 assists per game), he was selected to play in the 1988 All-Star Game. Rivers still shares the NBA single-game playoff record for most assists in one half with 15, which was achieved during a 1988 playoff game against the Boston Celtics.

JERRY SLOAN

Sloan attended McLeansboro Township High School, which is now located at 200 Jerry Sloan Ave., McLeansboro, Illinois. A native of McLeansboro, Illinois, he played college basketball at the University of Evansville, and then went on to play for the Chicago Bulls during the Bulls' formative years. He was the first player selected by the Bulls in the expansion draft, earning him the nickname "The Original Bull." Sloan was known for his tenacity on defense, and led the expansion team to the playoffs in its first season. Sloan enjoyed a respectable NBA career, playing in two All-Star Games, being named to the NBA All-Defensive First Team four times, and the All-Defensive Second team twice, and helping lead the Bulls to the playoffs on various occasions and helping them win one central conference title. Not someone to back off from contact and hustle, his career was cut short by injuries, and he turned his attention to coaching.

DOUG COLLINS

Collins enjoyed a successful high school basketball career at Benton High School in Benton, Illinois. In 1969, he went on to play for Illinois State University, close to where he grew up. He now has his own court named after him at Illinois State University's Redbird arena. He was chosen to represent the United States at the infamous 1972 Summer Olympics in Munich, Germany. While those games are mainly remembered for the terrorist attack that left several Iraeli athletes dead, there was also the controversial gold medal basketball game between the United States and the Soviet Union, in which Collins played a key part.

The United States was undefeated in Olympic basketball competition history, and widely expected to remain undefeated after those Olympics. After Collins had hit two free throws, the time had apparently expired in the gold medal game; the United States had a 50-49 lead and seemed to have secured yet another gold medal. However, in a very controversial move, it was decided by the game's referees that there were still three seconds left to play, allowing the Soviets one more chance, which they utilized to make a lay-up. This gave the U.S. its first ever Olympic loss by a 51-50 margin.

Collins made his NBA debut with the Philadelphia 76ers during the 1973-74 season. He only played 25 games his first year as a 76er, averaging 8 points per game. His numbers substantially improved over the next few seasons, scoring almost 18 points and dishing out 2.6 assists, while getting almost 4 rebounds per game in 81 games played during the 1974-75 season. And, then 20.8 points per game and grabbing four rebounds per game in 1975-76. He kept tallying an average of about 19 points and four rebounds per game for the next three seasons, as the 76ers reached the NBA finals during the 1976-77 season. Although the team featured Julius Erving, among others, the Sixers could not overcome Bill Walton and the Portland Trail blazers in those finals, losing four games to two.

During the 1978-79 season, Collins suffered a serious injury which limited him to only 47 games that year, and eventually forced him into retirement as a basketball player. His last season was 1980-81, in which he played only 12 games before announcing his retirement. Collins scored a total of 7,427 points in 415 NBA games, for an average of 17.9 points per game, while grabbing 1,339 rebounds for 3.2 per game, and passing for 1,368 assists, averaging 3.3 assists per game.

Collins later resurfaced as head coach of the Chicago Bulls from the middle to late 1980s, where he coached Michael Jordan. Although the Bulls had a string of playoff appearances during Collins' tenure, they were unable to win a Championship, and Collins was replaced by his assistant Phil Jackson. He was named the head coach of the Detroit Pistons in 1995, for whom he served until 1997 when he was fired at the end of the season and replaced by Alvin Gentry. Collins then became a television broadcaster, working for many years for various networks, such as NBC and TNT. He worked as a broadcaster for about five years, before being hired to coach again, by the Washington Wizards before the start of the 2001-02 NBA season. After the Wizards fired him following the 2002-03 season, Collins returned to announcing games for TNT.

LUTHER HEAD

Head attended Manley Academy in Chicago, Illinois, where he averaged over 20 points, eight assists and seven rebounds per game as a junior. Those numbers earned him All-City honors and he was selected MVP of the Blue Division of the Chicago Public League. Led by Head and head coach Bo Delaney, Manley had a perfect 12-0 record and won the conference championship in the Blue-West Division. Manley finished 26-7 overall, losing to state runner-up Chicago Westinghouse in the Public League quarterfinals. During the season, Head posted 10 triple-doubles. In a game against Chicago Wells, Head broke the city record and recorded the second-highest numbers in assists in a game with 25, earning Prep Player of the Week honors from the *Chicago Tribune.* During the IHSA State Playoffs, Head scored 26 points and contributed 15 assists against Marshall in a first-round victory. He would then post a triple-double in a second-round win over Steinmetz. During the summer, Head attended the Adidas ABCD Camp in New Jersey.

As a senior, Head averaged 22 points, eight rebounds, six assists and five steals in the rugged Red-West Division of the Chicago Public League. He would earn First-Team All-State honors in 2001 from the *Chicago Tribune, Chicago Sun-Times, Champaign-Urbana News Gazette,* Associated Press and illinois Basketball Coaches Association. He was also selected to play in the Wendy's All-Star Classic as a senior. He played primarily point guard in high school, but occasionally played shooting guard to complement his abilities. Head also finished sixth in the voting for Mr. Basketball in the state of Illinois following his senior year. However, to many scouts, Head's senior year was seen as a disappointment as a few of his statistics dropped since his junior year. Nevertheless, he would sign his letter of intent to play college basketball for the University of Illinois where he became the first Illinois recruit from the Chicago Public League since 1994.

At the University of Illinois, Head's senior year would be his finest. He was selected as a consensus Second-Team All-American, Associated Press Second-Team All-American, NABC Second-Team All-American, College Insider.com All-American, Sports Illustrated.com Honorable Mention All-American, First-Team All-Big Ten selection by both league coaches and media, Big Ten All-Tournament Team selection, NCAA Chicago Regional All-Tournament Team honoree, NCAA Final Four All-Tournament Team, Wooden Award finalist, Oscar Robertson (USBWA) Player of the Year finalist, Adolph Rupp Award finalist, Midseason Naismith Award candidate, USBWA All-District, and NABC First-Team All-District. Following the end of his senior season in 2005, Head automatically became eligible for the upcoming NBA Draft.

The draft workouts proved to be highly favorable for Head as scouts dubbed him one of the most improved players. On draft night the Houston Rockets selected Head with the 24th pick in the first round of the 2005 NBA Draft. Signed to a professional contract just days after being drafted, Head backed up the aging David Wesley. He has proven his worth as a valuable reserve, and has established himself as a reliable clutch shooter, making several game-clinching shots late in games.

Isiah Thomas

Isiah Lord Thomas III grew up in the heart of Chicago's West Side ghetto, the youngest of seven boys and two girls born to Mary and Isiah Thomas II. Eventually, Isiah II and Mary Thomas separated, and the child bearing duties fell primarily to Mary. Born a Baptist, she turned the family toward Catholicism and thus came under the wing of a local church, Our Lady of Sorrows, and its schools.

Thomas spent most of his free time playing basketball at tiny Gladys Park, next to Chicago's Eisenhower Expressway. Thomas was tutored by his older brothers, some of whom were top-notch players in their own right. When Thomas was 12, the street gangs began moving in more ferociously, and some of his older brothers succumbed to the lure of drug abuse and crime. Mary Thomas moved the family five miles west to Menard Avenue, but trouble seemed to follow.

Most of the coaches in the Chicago area considered Thomas too small to have any significant impact on a basketball program, but Thomas's brother persuaded coach Gene Pingatore of St. Joseph High School to give Isiah a sports scholarship. St. Joseph was located in a white suburb of Chicago. Thomas had to commute three hours each way to and from school, taking three buses and arriving home after dark. He struggled to acquire discipline in the classroom and on the court and, by his junior year, he led St. Joseph to a second-place finish in the state high school championship tournament. As a senior, Thomas was one of the most coveted college prospects in the nation.

More than 100 colleges recruited Thomas. His family wanted him to stay home and attend DePaul, but he chose to go to Indiana and play for temperamental coach Bob Knight. Thomas made All-Big Ten his freshman year and was named consensus All-American as a sophomore. That year he led Indiana to the NCAA championship game, which the Hoosiers routed the North Carolina Tar Heels, 63-50. With 23 points in the championship game, Thomas was named NCAA tournament Most Valuable Player. Despite his All-Star performance as a freshman and sophomore, Thomas was not happy at Indiana. He and Knight clashed frequently. Finally in 1981, on the advice of his friend Magic Johnson, Thomas decided to leave college and apply for the NBA draft.

Thomas was selected second in the opening round of the 1981 NBA Draft by the Detroit Pistons, a hopelessly foundering organization that had won only 37 of 164 games the previous two seasons. At the tender age of 19, Thomas became burdened with the chore of rescuing the NBA's worst team. Undaunted by the expectations, Thomas turned in a successful rookie season, averaging 17 points per game and leading the team in assists and steals. He improved in his second season, averaging nearly 23 points and 8 assists per game. Both years he represented the Pistons at the All-Star Game.

Throughout his first four years in Detroit, Thomas consistently outplayed his teammates. He was the first player in league history to be voted to the All-Star team in his first five season's, and in 1984 and 1986 his performances in the All-Star game were so spectacular that he was named the contest's Most Valuable Player. By 1984 he had managed to guide the Pistons to their first winning record in seven seasons, and he was given a new ten-year, $12 million contract that was specifically designed to keep him in Detroit for his entire career. He responded to this vote of confidence in the 1984-85 season by compiling an NBA-record 1,123 assists, an average of 13.1 per game.

With Isiah Thomas at the height of his ability, the Pistons won the championship in 1989 and again in 1990. These championship teams were often embroiled in controversy, both for their aggressive style of play and for their combative attitudes off-court. Thomas was named Most Valuable Player of the 1990 championship series. Thomas met many of the goals he set for himself as a rookie in the NBA, and exceeded even his own sky-high expectations. The leader in every category in the history of the Pistons' franchise, Thomas also left the game as the fourth all-time NBA leader in assists and steals, and the 28th all-time leader in scoring. Thomas retired with 18,222 career points, 9,061 assists, and 1,861 steals in 979 games. During the NBA's 50th Anniversary, he was named one of the 50 Greatest Players in NBA History. In 2000, Thomas was elected to the Basketball Hall of Fame, in his initial year of eligibilty.

JOHNNY ORR

Johnny grew up in the central Illinois town of Taylorville during the great depression. Orr attended Taylorville High School under Dolph Stanley and in his senior year led the Purple Tornadoes to a state championship and an undefeated season. After high school Orr went to the University of Illinois and was the youngest freshman to compete in three sports. After joining the United States Navy for the end of World War II, Orr returned to the college game at Beloit College.

Orr was originally drafted in the 1948 draft by the Minneapolis Lakers of the Basketball Association of America, the precursor to the NBA. Orr did not play for the Lakers, and was again drafted the next year in the 2nd round by the St. Louis Bombers. In 1950, Orr played 21 games for the Bombers before moving to the Waterloo Hawks for 13 more games.

DOH OHL

Ohl attended Edwardsville High School in Edwardsville, Illinois, and the nearby University of Illinois. Born in Murphysboro, Illinois, Ohl spent 10 seasons (1960-70) playing professional basketball in the NBA. Ohl played for the Detroit Pistons, Baltimore Bullets, and the St. Louis/Atlanta Hawks. Among the distance shooters of his time, the 6'3", 190-pound guard scored 11,549 points and appeared in five NBA All-Star Games in his career. His nickname was "Waxie," so called because of his short hair style.

Shortly after the 1963-64 champaign, Ohl was involved in one of the first so-called megatrades, this one an eight-player deal between the Pistons and the Bullets. On June 9, 1964, the Pistons sent Ohl, center Bob Ferry, forward Bailey Howell, forward Les Hunter and the draft rights to guard Wally (later Wali) Jones to the Bullets in exchange for forwards Terry Dischinger, Don Kojas and Rod Thorn. The deal turned out to be a fortuitous one for the Bullets, as Howell and Ohl became mainstays with the team.

Ohl experienced his finest hour in the 1965 playoffs, which saw the Bullets eliminate the St. Louis Hawks in four games in round one. In the Western Division finals, Ohl and future Hall of Fame guard Jerry West were locked in a tense shootout, that saw West and the Los Angeles Lakers finally prevail in six games, each of which was decided by eight points or fewer. Ohl averaged 26.1 points in 10 games that post-season.

DONNIE FREEMAN

A 6'3" guard, Freeman attended Madison High School and the University of Illinois before being selected by the Philadelphia 76ers in the third round of the 1966 NBA Draft. Freeman never played for the Sixers; he spent the first eight seasons of his professional basketball career in the ABA, playing for the Minnesota Muskies, Miami Floridians, Texas/Dallas Chaparrals, Utah Stars, Indiana Pacers, and San Antonio Spurs. He scored 11,544 points during his ABA career and appeared in five ABA All-Star Games, four as a starter. Freeman joined the NBA's Los Angeles Lakers in 1975. He spent one season with that club, averaging 10.8 points per game before retiring in 1976.

Freeman was the 5th player to score 10,000 points in an ABA career. He was a member of the 1972-73 Indiana Pacers ABA Championship team. He was a 4-time member of the ABA All-Pro Team. His second season in Miami he averaged 27.4 points per game. He became a perfect example of a guy given a chance to play by the new league and turning into a star. As a result of his fine play, he was selected a member of the ABA's All-Time Team.

DARRELL WALKER

Darrell Walker was born in Chicago, Illinois and attended Chicago's Corliss High School. After playing college basketball at Westark Community College and the University of Arkansas, Walker was selected by the New York Knicks with the 12th pick in the first round of the 1983 NBA Draft. Over a ten year career, he played for five teams; the Knicks, the Denver Nuggets, the Washington Bullets, the Detroit Pistons, and the Chicago Bulls.

Walker was selected to the 1984 NBA All-Rookie team, and was among the league leaders during his career in assists and steals. His best season was in 1989-90 with the Washington Bullets when he averaged 9.5 points, 8.8 rebounds and 8.0 assists per game. He won an NBA title with the Chicago Bulls in his final season.

Walker has served as head coach for two different NBA teams; the Toronto Raptors, and the Washington Wizards. He was the Raptors' second coach, following Brendan Malone, and led the team for a season and a half. In 2000, he replaced the fired Gar Heard in Washington for half a season (the first coaching "call up" in history, having previously been the coach of the Rockford Lightning of the CBA), but was then replaced by Leonard Hamilton the next year. Walker served as an assistant coach with the New Orleans Hornets, but has recently accepted an assistant coaching with the Detroit Pistons.

HERSEY HAWKINS

After starring at Westinghouse High School in Chicago, the 6'3" shooting guard attended Bradley University, where he averaged an NCAA Division I - high 36.3 points per game in 1988. He was then drafted by the Los Angeles Clippers in the first round of the 1988 NBA Draft, but his rights were immediately traded to the Philadelphia 76ers for the draft rights to Charles Smith. Hawkins earned NBA All-Rookie First Team honors in 1989, and in 1991 he averaged 22.1 points and appeared in the NBA All-Star Game. Hawkins was well known for his outside-shooting ability and his defensive skills. On the 76ers, "Hawk" was the second scoring option after Charles Barkley.

In 1993, Hawkins was traded to the Charlotte Hornets for Dana Barros, Sidney Green and draft picks, and after a productive two seasons in Charlotte, Hawkins, along with Hornet player David Wingate, were traded to the Seattle SuperSonics for Kendall Gill. In 1996, he played a key role. complimenting Gary Payton and Shawn Kemp on a Sonics team that made it to the NBA Championship before losing to the Chicago Bulls. He later joined the Bulls in 1999, but his one-year tenure in Chicago was marred by injury, and he only averaged 7.9 points per game. He returned to Charlotte in 2000 for his final season, and retired in 2001 with 14,470 career points and a ranking of 15 all-time in career NBA three-point field goals made. After retirement, Hawkins served as color analyst for Memphis Grizzlies Television alongside play-by-play man Matt Devlin. Hawkins along with Tyrone Amundsen, coached varsity basketball for the 2006-07 season at Estrella Foothills High School in Goodyear, Arizona.

CRAIG HODGES

Craig Hodges attended Rich East High School in Park Forest, Illinois. he then attended Califorins State University, Long Beach before beginning a professional career that included playing for the San Diego Clippers, Milwaukee Bucks, Phoenix Suns, and Chicago Bulls. He was drafted by the San Diego Clippers in the third round (2nd pick, 48th overall) of the 1982 NBA Draft. The 6'2" guard was most remembered during his Bulls years as part of the bench that led the team to the 1991 and 1992 NBA Championships.

Hodges became the second player (after Larry Bird) to win three consecutive Three Point Contests, in 1990, 1991, and 1992. He holds the single round scoring record with 25 points as of April, 2007, as well as the record for consecutive made shots at 19 (which was not in the same round as the 25 points). Later, Hodges played professionally in Italy with Clear Cantu, and after that, coached college basketball at Chicago State University and is now shooting coach for the Los Angeles Lakers.

RANDY BROWN

Randy Brown attended Collins High School in Chicago, Illinois. He attended the University of Houston for two seasons before transferring to New Mexico State, where he was twice named to the All-Big West Team and led his squad to a 23-6 record as a senior. That season, he averaged 12.1 points, 6.4 assists and 3.0 steals, while setting school records in the latter two categories. He was selected by the Sacramento Kings in the second round (31st overall) of the 1991 NBA Draft.

Randy Brown's hustle defense, and playmaking ability led him to stardom at New Mexico State and a career in the NBA. After four years with the Sacramento Kings he returned to his hometown of Chicago as a veteran free agent and won championship rings with the Bulls in 1996. 1997 and 1998. He led the Bulls in assists in the 1999-2000 season. In 1995-96, Brown appeared in 68 games as a reserve for the Bulls, primarily when Coach Phil Jackson wanted to turn up the pressure a notch. He filled the same role the next two seasons, appearing in 72 and 71 games and helping the Bulls win two more titles.

Following Michael Jordan's retirement, he was a starter for much of the 1998-99 season and posted career-highs in scoring, rebounding, assists, steals and minutes played. Injuries limited him to 59 games, all but four as a starter, in 1999-2000, when he led the Bulls in assists. Brown signed as a free agent with Boston in the summer of 2001, but was traded to Phoenix along with Joe Johnson, Milt Palacio and a future first round pick for Rodney Rogers and Tony Delk.

TOM HAWKINS

A 6'5" forward, Hawkins starred at Chicago's Parker High School (now Robeson) before playing at the University of Notre Dame, where he became the school's first African American basketball star and gained recognition in 1958 for his 43-point game against the United States Air Force Academy. He was then selected by the Minneapolis Lakers in the first round of the 1959 NBA Draft, and he would have a productive ten-year career in the league playing for the Lakers as well as the Cincinnati Royals as he registered 6,672 career points and 4,607 career rebounds.

After completing a 10-year career in the NBA, Hawkins spent 19 years as a local and national television and radio broadcaster. He co-hosted Mid-Morning Los Angeles on KHJ-TV for six years and Daybreak L.A. on KABC-TV for two years. Hawkins was also a sports anchor for four years on KNBC-TV, where he earned a Golden Mike Award as a member of the 5 o'clock new team. He was a network basketball analyst with Curt Gowdy and Jim Simpson for a 5-year period covering NCAA basketball. During his 14 years at KABC radio he served as sports director and created Dodger Forecast, Dodger Confidential and Baseball Spotlight. While there, he hosted Sports Talk and Dodger Talk.

He served as the Los Angeles Lakers player representative and was a member of the NBA player's labor negotiation team. One of the Nation's leading eclectics, Tommy Hawkins recently (7/2007) completed 18 years with the Los Angeles Dodgers serving as both Vice President of Communications and of External Affairs. In those capacities, Hawkins coordinated publicity, public relations, broadcasting, publications, community and governmental affairs. In business and education, Hawkins was active as a partner in the Beverly Hills public relations and advertising firm, Bishop Hawkins and Associates. A leader in the community, Hawkins is a member of the Board of Directors of the Center Theater Group, Los Angeles Sports Council, Children's Burn Foundation, and Friends of Jazz at UCLA. He also serves on the Advisory Board of the California State Long Beach Graduate School of Sports Management, as well as Pepperedine University's Sports Advisory Board.

MANNIE JACKSON

Excellence in basketball opened doors for Jackson, and a desire for a good education did the rest. He attended segregated schools as a young child, but he entered a newly-integrated Edwardsville High School in 1952, in Edwardsville, Illinois. As a star basketball player, Jackson combined with a group of high achievers including future NBA player Don Ohl and his close friend Governor Vaughn to make Edwardsville a basketball powerhouse. Jackson and Vaughn led Edwardsville to the state championship finals in 1956, the first and only time the school has made the finals. Even though Edwardsville lost to West Rockford 67-65, Jackson was named first team All-State. His basketball skills helped him earn a full scholarship to the University of Illinois, where he was joined by teammate Governor Vaughn.

Jackson and Vaughn were the first African American players to start for the University of Illinois varsity basketball team. In the mid-1950s they did not find Champaign a welcoming town. The racism was sometimes evident at basketball games. After one close match, a hostile Univesity of Kentucky audience sang "Bye Bye Blackbird" as Jackson and Vaughn exited the court. Jackson graduated from the University of Illinois in 1960 and traveled to New York to try out for the NBA. Although he became a starter in the National Industrial Basketball League, a semi-pro league, he failed to make the New York Knicks.

The Harlem Globetrotters, an alternative pro team invited Jackson to a tryout. The Globetrotters had been founded in the 1920s because African Americans were barred completely from professional basketball. For decades the team had been touring America and Europe, playing a comic style of basketball that relied on sophisticated ballhandling and a good bit of slapstick as well. The team was owned and run by Chicago native Abe Saperstein, and it didn't take him long to detect Jackson's special qualities. In 1964, Jackson left the Globetrotters and settled in Detroit, where he attended graduate school to study economics while working at General Motors and playing a little semi-pro basketball on weekends. In 1868, he accepted a position in the personnel department at Honeywell, Incorporated, a Minneapolis-based conglomerate best known for its manufacture of thermostats and other controls of energy, environmental, and industrial systems. This aggressive Fortune 500 company proved to be a good arena for Jackson's skills and ambitions.

By 1993, the Harlem Globetrotters had fallen upon hard times. Once a staple of television and live audience gatherings, the Globetrotters had lost many of their marquee stars of the 1960s and 1970s and had done little to update its routines. As a result, attendance at Globetrotters games declined sharply and the franchise faced possible bankruptcy. Jackson thought the Globetrotters had the potential to regain their status as an American icon and international entertainment venue. He put together a team of investors, with himself providing the majority of the capital, and purchased the franchise for about $6 million in 1993.

By any yardstick the Harlem Globetrotters are an American institution, instantly recognizable for their comic basketball antics and family-oriented exhibitions. The Globetrotters are also one of the oldest professional sports franchises in the country. Today, they are owned and run by Mannie Jackson, a Fortune 500 executive who was once a Globetrotter himself. Jackson is the only African American owner in major professional sports who can boast controlling interest in his team. He has used that power to rejuvenate the Globetrotters and position them for an even higher international popularity in the twenty-first century. Owning the Globetrotters is more than just a labor of love for Jackson, its a serious business venture, on which he expects to profit handsomely in years to come.

EMMETTE BRYANT

Emmette attended DePaul Academy High School in Chicago, Illinois. The 6'1" guard led the nation in scoring at 38.9 points per game while at Crane Junior College (now Malcolm X Community College). During his senior year at DePaul University, he broke his leg at the time when DePaul and UCLA were the only Division I colleges still unbeaten. He was picked in the 1964 NBA Draft by the New York Knicks.

Bryant played four seasons with the New York Knicks, teaming with Hall of Famer Willis Reed. He was then selected in the 1968 expansion draft by the Phoenix Suns. Phoenix traded him to the Boston Celtics for a second round draft choice on August 27, 1968. He won a championship with the Celtics following the 1968-69 season, the last of the Bill Russell Era. He was selected by the Buffalo Braves in the expansion draft and had career averages of 6.6 points, 2.8 rebounds and 3.0 assists per game.

RICKEY GREEN

A 6'0" guard, Rickey Green attended Hirsch High School in Chicago, and led the Huskies to the Class AA championship in 1973. In 1972, Hirsch advanced to the third round of the Public League playoff before losing to Carver. In 1973, Hirsch overcame a 20 point halftime deficit to beat DuSable and Mo Cheeks by one point in the city playoff, then edged Parker and Bo Ellis 55-53 in the city final to earn a trip to the Elite Eight in Champaign. Hirsch's only close call at state was a seven-point quarterfinal, after which the Huskies pressed on to the title, winning 65-51 over New Trier East.

Green attended one of the top junior college basketball programs in the nation, Vincennes (Indiana). Next he attended Michigan University and led the Wolverines to 1976 NCAA runner-up. He was drafted by the Golden State Warriors in the 1st round (16th pick overall) of the 1977 NBA Draft, which didn't turn out to be a good experience. Green went to the CBA and played in Hawaii for a year. He returned to the CBA and while playing in Billings, Montana then-general manager Frank Layden of the Utah Jazz noticed him and invited him to return to the NBA.

Rickey Green played professional basketball in the NBA for 14 seasons with eight teams. He was 38 when he retired in 1992, the oldest player was Robert Parish and he was second next to him. He never won an NBA championship. The highlight of his career was making the 1984 NBA All-Star team. He's currently serving as an assistant coach for the Philadelphia 76ers.

FLYNN ROBINSON

A 6'1" guard, Robinson attended Elgin High School in Elgin, Illinois. At Wyoming University, Robinson was a three-time All-Western Athletic Conference first team selection, averaging a conference-record 26.5 points a game. The 15th pick in the 1965 NBA Draft, he was an All-Star with the Milwaukee Bucks in the 1969-70 season, averaging a career-high 21.8 points per game while playing alongside rookie center Kareem Abdul-Jabbar. After the season, however, he was traded to the Cincinnati Royals in a deal that brought Oscar Robertson to the Bucks.

A year later to his delight, he was traded to the Los Angeles Lakers. What followed was a season for the ages, thirty three consecutive victories, the Lakers' all-time record that has never seriously been imperiled. Robinson helped the Lakers stamp into the record books during the 1971-72 season. The top-scoring reserve on that team that was unbeaten for two months and brought Los Angeles its first NBA title. As a backup to starters Jerry West and Gail Goodrich, the former Wyoming star averaged nearly 10 points in fewer than 16 minutes per game.

Robinson played seven seasons (1966-73) in the NBA and one season (1973-74) in the now-defunct American Basketball Association. He averaged 14 points per game and 3 assists per game during his professional career. Robinson led the NBA in free throw percentage in the 1969-70 season. In January 2005, Robinson was named to Wyoming's All-Century Team.

LLOYD WALTON

Lloyd Walton was born in Chicago, Illinois and he attended Mount Carmel High School on the city's South Side. He later attended Marquette University, where he played for legendary coach Al McGuire. Walton was drafted by the Miwaukee Bucks in 1976 and played for the Bucks from 1977 to 1980, and for the Kansas City Kings in 1980-81. A 6'0" guard, Walton played five seasons in the NBA.

DICK GARRETT

A 6'3" guard, Garrett attended Centralia High School in Centralia, Illinois. He played collegiately at Southern Illinois University and was selected by the Los Angeles Lakers with the 27th overall pick of the 1969 NBA Draft. He played five seasons (1969-1974) in the National Basketball Association, one with the Lakers, three with the Buffalo Braves, and his final season that he split between the New York Knicks and the Milwaukee Bucks. He earned NBA All-Rookie team honors during the 1969-70 NBA season after averaging 11.6 points per game for the Lakers.

ANDY PHILLIP

Born in Granite City, Illinois, Andy Phillip led Granite City to the 1940 Illinois State championship. A hot-shooting guard, Phillip the University of Illinois at Urbana-Champaign and was a member of the famed "Whiz Kids." Andy Phillip played for the Chicago Stags of the Basketball Association of America and the Philadelphia Warriors, Fort Wayne Pistons and Boston Celtics of the NBA.

Phillip was a guard/forward who had an 11 year professional career from 1948 to 1958. Phillip played in the first five NBA All-Star Games, and was twice named to the All-NBA Second Team. He led the NBA in assists during the 1950-51 and 1951-52 seasons. Phillip's teams made it to the NBA Finals during his final four seasons; twice with Fort Wayne and twice with Boston. The 1957 Boston team won the NBA Championship. He coached the St. Louis Hawks for 10 games in 1958, posting a 6-4 record. Phillip was elected to the Basketball Hall of Fame in 1961. Phillip died at his home in Rancho Mirage, CA on April 29, 2001. He was 79 years old.

BOBBY JOE MASON

Bobby Joe Mason attended Centralia High School in his native Centralia, Illinois. Following his all-star prep career at Centralia High School, Mason enjoyed a stellar career at Bradley University from 1956 through 1960, ending his career fourth on the school's all-time scoring list with 1,229 (23rd today). A two-time Helms Foundation All-American, Mason first earned the honor after helping the Braves to the first of four National Invitation Tournament Championships in 1957. A two-time, first-team All-Missouri Valley Conference selection in 1958 and 1959, Mason was voted to the Valley's all-time first-team in a 1970 league-wide fan vote.

Mason was twice selected in the NBA Draft, taken in the fifth round (36th overall) by the Minneapolis Lakers in 1959 and in the sixth round (41st overall) by the Cincinnati Royals in 1960. Mason opted instead to join the Harlem Globetrotters for whom he starred for 15 years from 1962 to 1976. During his tenure with the Globetrotters, Mason was named Most Valuable Player of the 1962 College Series and he was eventually elevated to team captain. He is listed as one of the organization's 23 "Legends" on the team's official website www.harlem-globetrotters.com.

SHAUN LIVINGSTON

Livingston, who played at Richwoods High School in Peoria, and then went to Peoria Central High School in Peoria, Illinois was highly touted as a high school recruit, earning comparisons to the great Magic Johnson. He led Peoria Central High School to Class AA state titles in 2003 and 2004. He was named *PARADE Magazine* All-America First Team. He played in the 2004 McDonald's High School All-American game and was named co-MVP. Livingston accepted a scholarship to Duke University, but later opted to forgo college and enter the 2004 NBA Draft, in which the Los Angeles Clippers selected him with the 4th overall pick in the ist round. He became the fourth Illinois Mr. Basketball to go straight to the NBA from high school (after Kevin Garnett, Darius Miles and Eddy Curry).

In his first two NBA seasons, playing a total of 91 games, Livingston averaged 6.3 points per game. In his third season, he scored a career high 9.3 points per game, being one of the few Clippers to improve from their amazing 2005-06 NBA season. Tragically, his break-out year was interrupted by a kneecap injury that led him to miss 39 games. Livingston then suffered a sickening broken leg injury on February 26, 2007 when he dislocated his left kneecap after land awkwardly following a missed layup. That result in his left knee snapping laterally, in a game against the Charlotte Bobcats. Livingston injured almost every part of the knee, tearing the anterior cruciate ligament (ACL), the posterior cruciate ligament (PCL), and the lateral meniscus while very badly spraining his medial collateral ligament (MCL), and dislocating his patella and his tibia-femoral joint. The damage was such that recovery will take 8 to 12 months to return, and he eventually missed the 2007-08 NBA season.

He was up and walking a couple of months later, but has been injury riddled for most of his professional career thus far. As a matter of fact, during the 2008 offseason, he became an unrestricted free agent when the Clippers did not extend him a qualifying offer and a spokes-person for the Los Angeles Clippers had stated that they have no intention of re-signing him. Later, it was learned that he was tendered a two-year contract with the club, but only to have Livingston turn it down. However, he did sign a two-year contract with the Miami Heat on October 3, 2008. A 6'7" point guard who can play both guard positions, Livingston is a tall ballhandler who has skills reminiscent of Lakers great, Magic Johnson.

DERRICK ROSE

As a freshman basketball player for John Calipari and the Memphis Tigers, Rose led them to the championship game of the NCAA Final Four. He was named to the All-Tournament Team, First-Team Conference USA, and Third-Team All-America. Rose is 6'3" and billed at around 200 pounds. He was considered the top point guard prospect of the 2007 high school class. During his college decision process, he also strongly considered the University of Illinois. His AAU team was the Mean Street Express. Rose goes by the nickname "Pooh," his grandmother called him that as a baby because he was fat and yellow like pooh bear. Tattooed on Rose's left bicep is a wizard holding a staff in one hand, a basketball in the other and framed by the words "The Great Poohdini." He owns two Illinois state championship rings. He has also been compared to current NBA star Dwyane Wade. Derrick Rose was picked 1st overall in the 2008 NBA Draft by the Chicago Bulls after declaring himself eligible for the 2008 NBA Draft following his freshman year.

Rose led Chicago Simeon to back to back Class AA state championships in Illinois. As a junior the Simeon all-stater made a great play on both ends of the court with a steal and eight-footer with one second left to lift Simeon to a 31-29 victory over Peoria Richwoods. He was All-Tournament First Team two consecutive years in 2006 and again in 2007 after leading Simeon to a 77-54 victory over O'Fallon in the title game. As a senior he was named to the McDonald's All-American Team and was a First Team All-American selection by *USA Today, Parade Magazine* and *EA Sports.* He averaged 25.2 points, 9.1 rebounds, 8,8 assists and 3.4 steals as a senior while leading Simeon to a 33-2 overall record. He was Illinois Mr. Basketball in 2007.

Rose has a rare combination of speed, elite athleticism and poise at the point guard position. He uses quickness and strength to power his way to the basket and can finish with incredible body control. He also makes good decisions with the basketball in the open court.

Dee Brown

Brown graduated from Proviso East High School in Maywood, Illinois, where he excelled not only athletically but also academically, finishing with a class rank of 16 out of 382 graduates. Brown was a star on Proviso East's basketball and football teams. He played quarterback for the football team, passing and rushing for more than 1,800 yards and 16 touchdowns in seven games during his senior season. His play at quarterback garnered the recruiting attention of many major collegiate football programs, including Florida State University and the University of Nebraska. His play on the basketball court, however, led Brown to be considered one of the best high school basketball players in the United States for his class. Brown was named Illinois Mr. Basketball and was a McDonald's All-American, and many recruiting analysts ranked him in the top 20 high school players.

Brown played at the University of Illinois from 2002 to 2006, receiving many awards and accolades. Brown was selected in the second round of the 2006 NBA Draft by the Utah Jazz. He played his rookie season with the Jazz, and then played for Galatasaray in the Turkish Basketball League. After the 2006 season, Brown was named Second-Team All-American by the Associated Press. Also, he was named the winner of the Bob Cousy Award for 2006, given to the nation's top collegiate male point guard.

He was first-team All-Big Ten, and a finalist for the John Wooden Award. But, on the last day of the 2008 NBA Las Vegas Summer League Brown was still trying to make a favorable impression on the Washington Wizards executives up in the stands. Brown has only a partially guaranteed contract from the Wizards. He has played in the national championship at Illinois, the Western Conference finals in his first NBA season, and the final four of the ULEB in Europe.

Shannon Brown

Brown attended Proviso East High School in Maywood, where his teammates included fellow 2006 draftee Dee Brown (no relation). In 2003, Shannon Brown was named Illinois Mr. Basketball and a McDonald's All-America. Brown played college basketball for the Michigan State Spartans. He was second-team All-Big Ten as a junior and was picked in the first round of the 2006 NBA Draft by the Cleveland Cavaliers and later traded to the Chicago Bulls. During the 2008 off-season, Shannon signed a contract to play with the Charlotte Bobcats.

FRANK WILLIAMS

Williams attended Manual High School in Peoria, Illinois. He helped his team win two IHSA class AA boys state basketball tournaments, in 1996 as a sophomore and again in 1997 as a junior. In both tournaments, Williams was named to the five-player All-Tournament team. As a senior, Williams was named the 1998 Illinois Mr. Basketball. After high school, Williams attended the University of Illinois, and played three seasons for the Fighting Illini, leading the team to a string of NCAA Tournament appearances. After the 2000-01 season, Williams was named Big Ten player of the year, and received the Chicago Tribune Silver Basketball award. As a point guard, Williams starred at both the high school and collegiate levels, but he has struggled to find a place in the NBA.

KENDALL GILL

Gill attended Rich Central High School in Olympia Fields, Illinois. Graduating in 1986, as a senior Gill led Rich Central to a 2nd place finish in the IHSA class AA boys basketball tournament. Gill led Rich Central in scoring with 54 points in the 4 games of the tournament finals, and was named to the six-player All-Tournament team.

After high school, Gill attended the University of Illinois. Playing four years for the Fighting Illini, Gill was a starter for his last three seasons. As a junior, Gill led the Fighting Illini to the 1989 Final Four. Also among the fabled "Flying Illini" squadron were future NBA players Nick Anderson, Marcus Liberty, Kenny Battle and Illini TV/Radio broadcaster Stephen Bardo. As a senior, Gill led the Big Ten in scoring and was named a first-teamAll-American (UPI). Gill left Illinois as the 7th all-time leading scorer in school history.

Gill was chosen in the 1990 NBA-Draft with the fifth overall pick by the Charlotte Hornets, and was named First Team All-Rookie for the 1990-91 season. Kendall also participated in a NBA Slam-Dunk competition. Gill played 15 seasons in the NBA for the Hornets (including two separate stints), Seattle SuperSonics, New Jersey Nets, Miami Heat, Minnesota Timberwolves, Chicago Bulls, and Milwaukee Bucks. In two different seasons Gill averaged over 20 points per game, first as a second-year plyer for the Hornets in 1991-92 (20.5 ppg), and again for the Nets in 1996-97 (21.8 ppg). In the 1997-98 NBA season, Gill led the league in steals as a member of the Nets. On April 3, 1999, he recorded 11 steals in a game against Miami, tying Larry Kenon's single-game record. Gill's career totals include 12,914 points in 966 regular season games. Gill was added to Comcast SportsNet's studio coverage of the Chicago Bulls as analyst prior to the 2006-07 NBA season. he Joins former Bulls guard Norm Van Lier and Mark Schanowski.

WILL BYNUM

Will Bynum averaged 11.8 points, 2.0 rebounds and 3.2 assists with the Detroit Pistons at the 2008 NBA Las Vegas Summer League. The 6-foot, 185-pound free agent point guard subsequently signed with Detroit and was added to the roster. He previously played for the NBA's Golden State Warriors. Prior to that he played for the Roanoke Dazzle of the NBA Development League, leading the league in scoring with 24.0 ppg. He was the 2005-06 league's Rookie of the Year.

After signing a contract with the Boston Celtics in the off-season of 2005, he participated in NBA preseason play and was subsequently waived before the start of the 2005-06 regular season. He signed with Maccabi Tel Aviv in Israel before the 2006-07 season and averaged 10.9 points, 1.9 rebounds, and 3.0 assists in two seasons with the club. Bynum is a playground legend in the Chicago area having outplayed many of the city's best players, including Antoine Walker, Tony Allen, Luther Head, Dee Brown, and Sean Dockery.

After starring at Crane High School in Chicago, he played for the University of Arizona in the NCAA before leaving for Georgia Tech. He never started at the University of Arizona and left the team after a disagreement with head coach Lute Olson. He helped Georgia Tech reach the Final Four, but lost to the Connecticut Huskies. Bynum hit the last second shot against Oklahoma State in the Final Four to propel the Yellow Jackets to the championship game.

QUINN BUCKNER

Buckner played basketball at Thornridge High School in Dolton, Illinois. His Falcons lost only one game during his junior and senior seasons and won back-to-back state titles. The 1972 Thornridge team is considered the best ever in Illinois high school history. The team was undefeated, with no team coming within 14 points of them. Buckner was also an excellent football player, making all-state in high school. He played basketball and football collegiately at Indiana University (football only two years) and seemed to get along with volatile Coach Bobby Knight better than any other player in the Hoosiers' history. Buckner was a starter and three-year captain at Indiana. As a senior in 1976 he co-captained the club to a 31-0 record and the NCAA championship.

He played for the United States men's national basketball team in the 1974 FIBA World Championship, winning the bronze medal. Although he scored only 10.0 points per game during his college career, Buckner was selected by the Milwaukee Bucks in the first round of the 1976 NBA Draft, the seventh pick overall. Before he joined the Bucks, Buckner played on the gold medal-winning 1976 U.S. Olympic basketball team alongside Adrian Dantley, Mitch Kupchak, and Scott May. But nothing prepared him for the NBA experience. Buckner's teams had suffered only 25 defeats in his eight years of high school and college basketball, and he had never been on a team that lost more than seven games in a season. But Milwaukee lost 52 times in 1976-77, finishing last in the Midwest Division.

Buckner established himself as a solid, dependable player with impeccable fundamentals. Milwaukee never did win the title. Boston, however, won the championship in 1984, with Buckner coming off the bench to spell Dennis Johnson and Gerald henderson. The Celtics went 62-20 during the regular season and then nudged the Loa Angeles Lakers in a seven-game NBA Finals. With the NBA championship ring, Buckner completed an impressive resume.

JEFF HORNACEK

He attended Lyons Township High School in LaGrange, Illinois, graduating in 1981. He led his team to the Illinois Sweet 16 in his senior year, coached by Ron Niksevich. He also playe shortstop on the baseball team. He redshirted at Iowa State University (ISU) in 1981, he was a campus walk-on from 1982 -1986, the son of a high school basketball coach became an all-conference player in the Big Eight Conference, playing for legendary coach Johnny Orr.

As a point guard, he guided the Cyclones to the Sweet 16 of the 1986 NCAA tournament. His best moment came at the Metrodome in Minneapolis, Minnesota when, after first hitting a shot to tie the game and send it to overtime, Jeff hit the game winning shot in overtime, a 26-ft jumper at the buzzer, to give ISU its first tournament win since 1944, beating Miami (Ohio), March 14, 1986, 81-79. Ron Harper was the starting shooting guard for Miami. Two days later, he led the Cyclones to the NCAA Tournament Sweet 16, in a 72-69 upset of second seed Michigan. Hornacek left ISU with a Big Eight record of 665 career assists, still an Iowa State school record, and 1,313 career points.

He was the 22nd pick in the 2nd round (46th overall) of the 1986 NBA Draft, by the Phoenix Suns. He became a star on the Suns, but after his sixth and most productive season, he was traded (along with Andrew Lang and Tim Perry) to the Philadelphia 76ers for Charles Barkley. With Hersey Hawkins, the Sixers' leading scorer in the shooting guard position, Hornacek was assigned point guard responsibilities. Although he had a career high 6.9 assists per game in his only complete season with the Sixers (192-93 season), his stint as a point guard was not a success (26 wins, 56 losses). Midway through the 1993-94 season (February 24), he was traded to the Utah Jazz for Jeff Malone, where he would return to his natural shooting guard position alongside point guard John Stockton.

Hornacek was one of the best in the NBA in moving without ball on offense. He was an instrumental part of the Jazz's drive to the NBA Finals in 1997 and 1998, where the Jazz lost to the Chicago Bulls both times. He remained with the Jazz until knee problems forced him to retire in 2000. Hornacek's #14 jersey was retired by the Utah Jazz, for whom he played from 1994 to 2000. Hornacek was recently hired by the Jazz to be a part-time assistant coach and to help Andrei Kirilenko with his shooting. He was known primarily as one of the last consumate shooters in the league.

TONY ALLEN

Allen attended Crane High School in Chicago, where he was a basketball standout. A 6 ft 4in and 213 lb shooting guard, he played for Oklahoma state University, where he was named the Big 12 Conference Player of the Year his senior year, after averaging 16 points per game and leading his team to the Final Four. He became the first player in OSU history to score 1,000 career points in just two seasons. He graduated from Oklahoma State with a degree in Education. After graduating, he declared himself ready for the 2004 NBA Draft.

Allen was selected by the Boston Celtics with the 25th overall pick of the 2004 NBA Draft. In his rookie season he averaged 6.4 points and 2.9 rebounds per game, and ranked 3rd in the league in steals per 48 minutes, with 2.89. He was selected to play for the rookies in the Got Milk? Rookie Challenge during All-Star Weekend, along with fellow Celtics Al Jefferson.

On January 10, 2007 in the final minutes of a Celtic loss to the Indiana Pacers, Allen suffered a debilitating knee injury as he landed awkwardly after an unnecessary slam dunk attempt, after the whistle had blown tearing the ACL, after twisting and bending his left knee during a hard landing, and had to be carried off the court. Allen underwent a successful anterior cruciate ligament reconstructive surgery on January 13 and was out for the rest of the season. He was averaging 11.5 points, 3,8 rebounds and 1.48 steals in 33 games. He played sparing during the 2007-08 season as the Celtics won their 17th NBA championship. However, Allen has resigned with the Celtics and is expected to be an integral part of the team as Boston prepares to defend their championship after having fully recovered from the injury.

CAZZIE RUSSELL

Russell wanted to be a major league baseball player. But Larry Hawkins discovered the 6-foot-2 freshman in a gym class and projected that he would grow to 6-foot-5. As a Sophomore, he led Carver High School to the Chicago Public League's frosh-soph championship. He led the varsity to the city semifinals as a junior, and emerged as the state's premier player in 1962, leading Carver to a 28-5 record and second place in the state tournament. A survey in the *Chicago Sun-Times* recently rated Cazzie as the No. 1 high school basketball player ever produced in the Chicago area.

Russell played college basketball at the University of Michigan, where he led the Wolverines to three consecutive Big Ten Conference titles (1964-66) and to Final Four appearances in 1964 and 1965. In 1966, Russell averaged 30.8 points per game and was named the College Basketball Player of the Year. Crisler Arena which opened in 1967, has been dubbed *The House that Cazzie Built.* Russell's number 33 jersey has been retired by the Wolverines.

Russell spent twelve seasons in the NBA (1966-1978), and is best remembered for his five seasons with the New York Knicks (1966-71). Russell was the NBA's first pick overall in the 1966 NBA Draft, and was named the the 1967

All-Rookie Team. He was part of the famous 1970 Knicks team that won the NBA championship over the Los Angeles Lakers. Russell played in the 1972 NBA All-Star Game while with the Golden State Warriors.

In 1981, he returned to pro basketball as a coach in the Continental Basketball Association for the Lancaster (Pa.) Lightning. He guided his team to that league championship that season. During the playoffs, with his team depleted by injuries, Russell came out of retirement and played for the Lightning in the final game of the league championship series, played in Lancaster, PA. As of the 2005-06 basketball season, Cazzie Russell coaches basketball at the Savannah College of Art and Design.

NICK ANDERSON

Anderson was a basketball standout at Simeon Vocational and Prosser Vocational High Schools in Chicago. He earned Mr. Basketball in Illinois honors, leading Simeon to the city championship and a No.1 national ranking in *USA Today* as a senior. He played collegiately at the University of Illinois. He played in the 1989 Final Four on the "Flying Illini" squad along with Kendall Gill, Marcus Liberty, Kenny Battle, and Stephen Bardo.

Anderson was the first pick in the history of the Orlando Magic. The University of Illinois star had the skills and the temperament to mesh with players elected in the expansion draft. Subsequently, the Orlando Magic selected him with the 12th pick overall in the 1989 NBA Draft. He wore No.25 in honor of his late friend and teammate, Ben Wilson. He is Orlando career scoring leader, and was the last original Magic player to leave, playing 10 seasons with the club. After 10 years with Orlando, the team traded him and he spent two years in Sacramento and one in Memphis before retiring after the 2001-02 season. As a matter of fact, to this day, Nick Anderson still holds a number of records for the Magic. He's first in games played (692), minutes played (22,448), points (10,650), and steals (1,004). He's second in rebounds (3,667) behind Shaquille O'Neal, and fourth in assists (1,937) behind Scott Skiles, Anfernee Hardaway, and Darrell Armstrong.

A starter for almost all of his career in Orlando, he emerged as the top scorer the year before Shaquille O'Neal was drafted. With the addition of O'Neal and Anfernee Hardaway in consecutive drafts, Anderson, along with Dennis Scott, became effective outside scoring options for the Magic, complimenting O'Neal's inside play and Hardaway's all-around game tremendously. Anderson lead the team in three-pointers made in 1994-95, hitting 179 and averaging just under 16 points per game. The Magic won 57 games, finished with the best record in the Eastern Conference, and won their first Atlantic Division title.

Anderson is well known for his role in sports psychology. After missing four pivotal free-throws in the 1995 NBA Championships that led to the defeat of the Orlando Magic by the Houston Rockets, Anderson developed a psychological problem that greatly affected his free throw shooting. His free throw percentage dipped sharply and dropped to 40% at one point. He had developed a fear of shooting free throws as a result of his belief that his missed free throws in the NBA

Finals caused the Magic to lose. This was an anomaly as he was considered a great shooter. After the helped of sports psychologists, Anderson improved his free throw shooting but showed signs of his fear again during the last year of his NBA career.

On March 10, 2006 the Orlando Magic held a tribute to Nick Anderson during a home game against the Cavaliers. While many Magic fans have voiced their desire for Anderson's #25 to be retired, the Magic seems unwilling and the aforementioned tribute appears to be as far as they'll go.Currently, the team has yet to retire the jersey of any former player. Anderson is now retired from basketball, but recently accepted a job with the Magic in the community realtions department.

TROY HUDSON

Troy Hudson, a 6'1" point guard, led Carbondale High School to second place in the IHSA Class AA boys' basketball tournament in 1994. He was the tournament leading scorer averaging over 27 points per game and made the All-Tournament First Team. After a college career at the University of Missouri and Southern Illinois University, Hudson was not drafted in the NBA draft.

Since earning a hard fought spot on the Utah Jazz in 1998, he later played for the Los Angeles Clippers and the Orlando Magic. However, his most productive seasons have come in Minnesota, where he averaged a career high 14.2 points, and 5.7 assists per game in 2002-03. Since landing a nice contract extension in 2003, Hudson had been plagued by nagging injuries that has hurt his production in recent years. He has averaged 9.2 points per game throughout his career. He was recently a reserve guard with the Golden State Warriors, but they have waived him.

DWIGHT "DIKE" EDDLEMAN

As a high school player, Eddleman is considered one of the finest players in the history of high school basketball in the state of Illinois. Eddleman played four years at Centralia High School, from 1939 to 1942. Eddleman led the Centralia Orphans to the 1942 Illinois state basketball championship, following finishing fourth in 1939 and third in 1941. In the 1942 title game, Eddleman single-handily led a comeback as the Orphans were 13 points down with five minutes to play. As a junior and senior, Eddleman led the state in scoring with 969 and 834 points respectively. His 969 points as junior easily the previous state record of 751. During his high school career, Eddleman scored 2,702 career points, which was at the time of his graduation from high school a state record for most points in a career. Eddleman was the first high school player in Illinois to average at least 20 points per game.

At the University of Illinois, Eddleman played for coach Harry Combes on the teams known as the "Whiz Kids." In 1949, Eddleman led the men's basketball team to the Big Ten title, and an appearance in the NCAA Final Four. That year, he earned the *Chicago Tribune's* Silver Basketball award as the conference MVP. He was named First Team All-American in 1949, and Second Team All-American in 1948. Eddleman was named First Team All-Big Ten in 1948, and Second Team All-Big Ten in 1949, and was the team MVP that year.

After leaving the University, Eddleman played professionally for four seasons in the National Basketball Association. In 1950, Eddleman led the Tri-Cities Blackhawks in scoring as a rookie. After playing one more season for the Blackhawks, Eddleman played two seasons for the Fort Wayne Pistons. Eddleman played in the NBA All-Star Game in both 1951 and 1952. Over his NBA career, Eddleman scored 3,221 points in 226 games, for a scoring average of 12.1 points per game.

As a high scholl athlete, Eddleman won three Illinois state high jump titles. As a collegian, he won an NCAA high jump championship in the high jump at the 1948 Summer Olympics in London. Eddleman participated in the 1947 Rose Bowl as a punter, and played a number of roles for the team in his career. As of the 2004 season, Eddleman maintains the Illinois team record for both the longest punt and the longest punt return. He's generally considered the greatest athlete in the history of athletics at the University of Illinois. In 1993, the University of Illinois athlete of the year awards for both men and women were named in his honor. In 2002, the portion of Fourth Street in Champaign, Illinois that runs along the east side of Memorial Stadium between Peabody Drive and Kirby Street was designated Honorary Dike Eddleman Way.

Anthony Parker

Parker started out playing high school at Naperville Central High School in Naperville, Illinois. He then played college basketball at Bradley University, where he established himself as a top player, averaging 18.9 points per game and shooting 42% from the three point line in his third season. He earned the Missouri Valley Conference (MVC) MVP and All-MVC first team honors in that season. His outstanding performances fo the Braves ensured that he became one of 15 players honored in Bradley's All-Century basketball team named in 2003.

Parker entered the 1997 NBA Draft after four years at Bradley and was selected 21st overall by the New Jersey Nets, but he was immediately traded to the Philadelphia 76ers in a multi-player trade. In his two seasons with the 76ers, Parker was largely plagued by injury and played in only 39 regular season games, averaging just over five minutes a game and totaling 74 points and 26 rebounds. He was subsequently traded with Harvey Grant to the Orlando Magic for Billy Owens before the 1999-2000 season. Parker again struggled at Orlando, playing only 16 games with modest averages of 3.6 ppg and 1.7 rpg before being released in January 2000. He finished the remainder of the season with the Quad City Thunder of the Continental Basketball Association where he averaged 11.5 points in 26 games.

Disappointed in his failure to make a breakthrough in the NBA, Parker turned to Europe to resurrect his basketball career, intending to return to the NBA after a good season with a European club. Eventually he moved to Israel in the

2000-01 season, where he signed with Israel powerhouse Maccabi Tel Aviv. Parker left Israel in 2002 and in January 2003 moved to Italy, where he signed with Virtus Roma, playing in 27 Serie A League games and averaging 14,5 ppg and 5.6 rpg. However, half a year later Parker longed to return to Israel. Back with Maccabi, he helped his team accomplish two more triple-feats by winning the Israel domestic championship, the Israeli National Cup, and the Euroleague championship in both 2004 and 2005. After six years of success in Europe however, Parker dreamt of returning to the NBA.

On October 2005, in a pre-season game representing Maccabi against the Toronto Raptors, Parker hit the game-winning shot with less than a second remaining lead Maccabi to a 105-103 win at Air Canada Centre. This gave the Raptors fans and management a glimpse of his abilities and in July 2006, Parker was officially signed by Raptors General Manager Bryan Colangelo as a free agent as part of a massive revamp of the 2006-07 Toronto team. Overall, in his first season with Toronto, he averaged 12.4 ppg, 3.9 rpg, and 2.1 apg, leading the team in three point field goals and free throw percentage. Parker's defensive and offensive versatility were credited as instrumental in helping the Raptors clinch their first-ever division title, first NBA Playoffs berth in five years, as well as best regular season record in franchise history.

ANDRE WAKEFIELD

Andre Wakefield attended Crane High School in Chicago. He was a 6'2 1/2" guard and played collegiately at the College of Southern Idaho and Loyola University Chicago. He played briefly in the NBA from 1978 to 1980. Wakefield was selected with the 19th pick in the fifth round of the 1978 NBA Draft by the Phoenix Suns. In two seasons with three different teams (Detroit Pistons, Chicago Bulls, Utah Jazz), he averaged 2.3 points, 1.0 rebounds, and 0.9 assists per game. After his playing days he became an assistant coach at Loyola.

EDDIE HUGHES

Hughes attended Austin High School in Chicago and was an all-state basketball player. He played collegiately at Colorado State University from 1978 to 1982. Hughes was a 5'10" point guard and was selected in the seventh round by the San Diego Clippers of the 1982 NBA Draft. His playing career in the NBA commenced in 1987-88 with the Utah Jazz, for whom he played 11 games, averaging 1.5 points and 0.7 assists per game. He then played a total of 86 games with the Denver Nuggets in his second and third seasons, his last being in 1990.

JANNERO PARGO

A 6'1" point guard, Pargo played high school basketball at Robeson High School (formerly Parker) in Chicago. He played collegiately for the University of Arkansas after transferring from Neosho County Community College in Chanute,

Kansas. He went undrafted in the NBA Draft in 2002, however, he worked hard and made the Los Angeles Lakers roster. He also played for the Toronto Raptors and the Chicago Bulls. He recently played for the New Orleans Hornets as a reserve, but currently plays point guard for Dynamo Moscow in Russia after signing a one year contract with the club.

He averaged 14.4 points and 2.8 assists in 60 games at the University of Arkansas, and was named Third Team All-Southeastern Conference in both his seasons while a Razorback. He averaged 18.0 points over two seasons at Neosho County CC. The 2006-07 season Pargo played in a career-high 82 games, averaged career-highs in points (9.2), rebounds (2.2) and assists (2.5) for the Hornets. He was the only Hornet to appear in every game. He led the team in points seven times and in rebounds once. He was second on the team in free throw percentage (852.) and three pointers made (81).

SAM MACK

Sam Mack was born in Chicago, Illinos and played high school basketball at Thornridge High School in neighboring Dolton, Illinois. The 6'7" shooting guard from the University of Houston played with five different NBA teams over a 7 year career. Since 2001, he has played in the Continental Basketball Association and also with Calpe Aguas of the Spanish League. Mack was selected in the 2005 All-American Professional Basketball League Draft, but the league folded soon thereafter. He averaged 7.8 points per game during his NBA career, while playing in 259 games.

STEPHEN BARDO

Stephen Bardo attended Carbondale High School in Carbondale, Illinois. A 6'5", 190 lb guard, Bardo had a standout career at the University of Illinois, which included an appearance in the 1989 NCAA men's basketball tournament Final Four. He scored 909 points and compiled many assists for the Fighting Illini. He was selected in the 1990 NBA Draft by the Atlanta Hawks, but never played for them. Instead, he spent time in the Continental Basketball Association before joining the San Antonio Spurs during the 1991-92 NBA season.

Bardo also played for the Dallas Mavericks, Detroit Pistons and teams in France, Italy, Japan, Spain, and Venezuala before joining ESPN in August 2000, where he currently works as a color commentator for basketball games. Bardo also works as a sports reporter for Chicago's WBBM-TV (CBS Channel 2), and he is an analyst for the Illini Sports Network, which broadcasts University of Illinois sporting events.

DONNIE BOYCE

Boyce was born in Chicago, Illinois and played high school basketball at Proviso East High School in neighboring Maywood, Illinois, along with future NBA draft picks Michael Finley and Sherrell Ford. Boyce played collegiately at the University of Colorado and was selected with the 13th pick in the 2nd round of the 1995 NBA Draft by the Atlanta Hawks. He played for the Hawks for parts of two seasons from 1996 to 1997, averaging 2.6 points in 30 games. Boyce later played in the CBA for the Albany Patroons. He has also played basketball for the Harlem Globetrotters.

RONNIE FIELDS

Ronnie Fields was born in Chicago, Illinois and played at Farragut Academy in Chicago from 1992-1996. He was a teammate of Kevin Garnett during the 1995 season. Fields had a (reported) 50-inch vertical leap. He was a 3-time Parade All-American selection (1994-96) and a consensus First Team All-American (Parade, USA Today, McDonald's) his senior year. He was also the first sophomore to ever play in the "Best of the Best" game at the Nike All-American camp in 1993, a game that featured Allen Iverson, Kevin Garnett, and Naismith Prep Player of the Year winners Ron Mercer and Jerod Ward.

In high school he averaged 32 points, 12 rebounds, 4 assists, and 4 blocks a game. A 6'3" guard, Fields was injured in a car accident on February 26, 1996, in which he broke his neck. He had to wear a protective halo while his neck healed. It is believed that Ronnie had a total of 372 dunks in his high school career. He left high school as the third all-time leading scorer in Chicago Public League history with 2,619 points. His high school teammates include Garnett (95), Arizona Wildcat forward Michael Wright (98) and Willie Farley (95).

Ronnie signed a letter of intent at DePaul University in his hometown, but was later ruled academically ineligible. He declared himself eligible for the 1996 CBA Draft and was selected in the 7th round (73rd overall) by the LaCrosse Bobcats. He also declared for the 1997 NBA Draft but later withdrew his name. Fields was eligible for the 1998 NBA Draft but went undrafted. Fields is considered by many to be one of the greatest dunkers of all-time at any level of basketball. A fantastic slasher, he was CBA steals leader several times, and is the only player in the history of the CBA to lead the league in both scoring and steals in two straight seasons.

KIWANE GARRIS

Kiwane Garris was born in Chicago, Illinois and was an outstanding basketball player at Westinghouse High School on the city's West Side. Garris played college basketball at the University of Illinois. He is a 6'2", 183 lb point guard. As a freshman in the 1993-94 season, Garris led the team in scoring and free-throw percentage. Garris also led the team in assists in the 1994-95 and 1996-96 seasons. Garris finished his career at Illinois as the second all-time leading scorer, behind former teammate Deon Thomas. Garris finished with 1,948 career points, with a career scoring average of 16.8 points per game.

He played for the US national team in the 1998 FIBA World Championship, winning the bronze medal. He has also played with the Grand Rapids Hoops of the CBA, Italian teams Banca Popolare Ragusa (Serie A2, 2003-04), Porte Garofoli Osimo (Serie A2, 2002-03), Bipop-Carire Reggio Emilia (Serie A2, 2003-04, Serie A, 2004-05), Climamio Bologna (2005-06) (reached the Italian championship final and won the Italian Supercup) and Armani Jeans Milano (2006-07). He played in the NBA for the Denver Nuggets (1997-98, 28 games, 8 mpg, 2.45 ppg) and the Orlando Magic (1999-2000, 3 games, 7.7 mpg, 1.3 ppg). He has been signed for a brief period by the Los Angeles Clippers (1997 preseason) and the Sacramento Kings (2002 preseason), but was waived before the regular season began in both cases and has not played any NBA games for those clubs. He's currently playing basketball for Premiata Montegranaro of the Italian league.

CHAPTER SEVEN

GREAT FORWARDS

QUENTIN RICHARDSON

Quentin Richardson arrived at DePaul University after leading Whitney Young High School, in Chicago, to the state AA basketball title in 1998. He averaged 17.9 points per game, and 10.2 rebounds per game in his two seasons at DePaul. He became the only player in school history to have 1,000+ points, 500+ rebounds, and 100+ three-point field goals. As a freshman, he was elected both Conference USA Player of the Year, and Freshman of the Year. Richardson declared for the NBA Draft after his sophomore year with DePaul in 2000.

He was named the 1998 high school basketball Player of the Year by *USA Today*. He was named the 1999 Player of the Year by the Chicago Sun-Times. He was also a MCDonald's All-American. The 2004-05 season was a big one not only for Richardson, but the Phoenix Suns as well. He set a new Suns single-season record for three-point field goals, eclipsing the previous record of 199 set by Dan Majerle. He finished the season with a league-leading 631 three-point attempts, and 226 three-point field goals, co-leading the league with Kyle Korver. Richardson also set a Suns franchise record with nine threes against the New Orleans Hornets on December 29, 2004. Richardson went on to win the NBA All-Star Three-Point Shootout that same season. Richardson currently plays in the NBA for the New York Knicks.

TERRY CUMMINGS

A graduate of Carver High School, in Chicago, Cummings attended DePaul University from 1979 to 1982. He averaged 16.4 points per game over 85 games and entered the 1982 NBA Draft after departing from school. He was selected in the first round by the San Diego Clippers, and in his inaugural 1982-83 season, he won the NBA Rookie of the Year Award after putting up 23.7 points and 10.4 rebounds per game. In 18 seasons Terry Cummings, a reliable power forward, scored 19,460 points. He finished with averages of 16.4 points per game and 7.3 rebounds per game. The 2-time All-Star also played in 1,183 games, had 33,898 minutes, a .484 field goal percentage (3,326 for 4,711), 8,630 total rebounds (3,183 offensive, 5,447 defensive), and 1,255 steals.

Cummings is an ordained Penecostal Minister and performed service at the wedding of former teammate, Sean Elliott. Terry has three sons, Antonio, TJ, and Shawn. TJ Cummings recently played in the NBDL for the Albuqueque Thunderbirds. In a creative turn of his career, Cummings released an album, "T.C.

Finally" in early 2007, of songs which he wrote, sang, and played keyboards. The album is reminiscent of R&B/Soulstyles of musicians such as Marvin Gaye, Al Green, and Sam Cooke.

MARK AGUIRRE

A graduate of Westinghouse High School, in Chicago, Aguirre was a high-profile player for many years. A powerful 6-foot-6 forward with an uncanny jumper, a catalog of offensive tricks, and confidence to try for challenging shots, he filled up the scoring column for much of his 13-year NBA career. A college standout at DePaul University, he averaged 24.5 points over three with the Blue Demons, and in 1981 was *The Sporting News'* College Player of the Year. He was also the USBWA College Player of the Year and James Naismith Award winner in 1980. He's also a two-time member of *The Sporting News'* All-American first team. As a freshman in 1978-79, he led the Blue Demons to the Final four, where they lost to Indiana State, led by future NBA Hall of Famer Larry Bird.

One of the NBA's most flashy and prolific scorers during the 1980s, Aguirre a 3-time NBA All-Star, averaged 20 points per game over the course of his 13-year NBA career. He was selected as the first overall pick by the Dallas Mavericks in the 1981 NBA Draft and remained with the Mavericks until 1989. His greatest season came in 1983-84, when he averaged 29.5 points per game, second in the league. He finished the season with 2,330 total points. Both Mavericks single-season records still stand. He retired in 1994 after helping the Detroit Pistons win back-to-back championships in 1989 and 1990. As of 2006, he ranks 45th in the all-time scoring list, with 18,458 points.

JULIAN WRIGHT

Julian Wright played high school basketball at Homewood-Flossmoor High School in Flossmoor, Illinois. In 2005 he was selected to the McDonald's All-American team, and he was rated among the top ten basketball players in his class by several recruiting services due to his talent and versatility. At 6'8" and 225 lbs, Wright combines good size with excellent athleticism and skills, which allowed him to play numerous positions in high school, including point guard, small forward, and power forward.

Wright entered the 2005-06 NCAA season for the Kansas Jayhawks as the pre-season freshman of the year in the Big 12 Conference. Though he didn't start at the beginning of the season, he quickly played his way into the starting power forward slot. His superior athleticism often allowed him to score baskets simply by virtue of having beaten the defense down the court. During his freshman season, Wright averaged 8.5 points per game, but he was praised for his ability to help his team without scoring. He was named to the All-Big 12 Tournament Team and the All-Big 12 Freshman Team along with fellow Kansas freshman Brandon Rush and Mario Chalmers. In 2007, he was again placed on the All-Tournament team.

For his play during the 2006-07 season, Wright was named a third team All-American by the National Association of Basketball Coaches' All American Team. Wright announced that he was making himself eligible for the 2007 NBA Draft. He was selected by the New Orleans Hornets as the 13th overall selection of the 2007 NBA Draft.

SONNY PARKER

Parker attended Farragut High School in Chicago, Illinois, where he received All-City, All-State, and All-Public League honors. In appreciation of his efforts on the school's basketball team, he was named to the Farragut Hall of Fame, the Chicago Public Schools Hall of Fame, and the Illinois High School Hall of Fame. After graduating from high school, Parker spent two years at Mineral Area College. In both of his seasons, Parker was named All-American, as well as Conference Player of the Year and Region Player of the Year. He was an All-Conference and All-Region pick, and is the Mineral Area College's leading career scorer. He has been inducted into the Junior College Hall of Fame.

Although Parker was recruited by many of the top college basketball programs, he chose to attend Texas A&M University, primarily to learn under legendary coach Shelby Metcalf. In his two years at Texas A&M, Parker led the Aggies to back to back Southwest Conference titles, earning himself first-team All-Southwest Conference honors both years as well. The team reached the NCAA Tournament in 1974-75. As a senior, Parker averaged 20.7 points per game, a feat only two othe Aggie players have achieved in 20 years since he left. He has been inducted into the Texas A&M Athletic Hall of Fame.

Parker was a first-round draft pick, chosen by the Golden State Warriors as the 17th pick in the 1976 NBA Draft. For 29 years, Parker held the record as the highest an Aggie had ever been drafted, until 2005 Antoine Wright was chosen as the 15th overall draft pick by the New Jersey Nets. For the six years that he played professional basketball, Parker averaged 9.9 points, 4.1 rebounds, and 3.7 assists per game, with 144 steals and 33 blocks. In 1990, Parker established the non-profit Sonny Parker Youth Foundation (SPYF) in his hometown of Chicago, Illinois. The foundation is designed to provide year-round educational, recreational, multi-cultural programs for inner-city children from kindergarten through 12th grade. Parker is president of the organization and is active in its daily activities.

MAURICE "BO" ELLIS

Ellis is Chicago native and a former prep All-American at Parker High School (now Paul Roberson) on the city's South Side. In 1973 he was selected by *Parade Magazine* as high school Co-Player of the Year. He was also a three-time Chicago Public League, All-Area, All-City, and All-State selection during his high school years. He was selected into the Chicago Public League and Illinois High School Coaches Hall of Fame.

As a player, Bo Ellis was recognized as one of the best athletes during his collegiate days at Marquette University. As captain of the Marquette Warriors, Ellis led his team, coached by the legendary Al McGuire, to the 1977 National Championship. Ellis was selected to the All-American team each of his four years in college, was a member of the 1977 NCAA Final Four All-Tournament Team and was invited to participate in the 1976 USA Olympic Tryouts. He remains the second leading rebounder and fourth leading scorer in Marquette University's history. A durable athlete, Ellis played 120 consecutive games in his four years at Marquette. In 1992, Marquette retired his jersey number, and he's in the Marquette University Hall of Fame.

In 1977, he was drafted as a first round choice by the Washington Bullets. He was later traded and played for the Denver Nuggets until 1980. He then played professionally in Italy, Switzerland and Belgium until 1983. In 1998, Ellis joined the Chicago State University Intercollegiate Athletic Department as head Men's Basketball Coach. With one of the least funded athletic departments in the NCAA's Division I Mid-Continent Conference, Coach Ellis is responsible for assembling a team of bright and talented student-athletes that will regain the recognition and esteem that CSU's basketball team once had.

ANDRE IGUODALA

A graduate of Lanphier High School in Springfield, Illinois, Iguodala, a 6'6", 207 pound swingman was selected 9th overall in the 2004 NBA Draft out of the University of Arizona. He was named first team All-Rookie in 2005 and started on the rookie team during the Rookie Challenge portion of All-Star Weekend. Iguodala played at Arizona two years and in the 2003-04 seasaon collected three triple-doubles, joining Jason Kidd as the only two players in Pac-10 history to post two or more triple-doubles in the same season.

During his first year with the Philadelphia 76ers, he was the only team member to play and start all 82 games plus 5 playoff games. Iguodala is known for his athleticism and already holds a reputation as a strong defender. Andre Iguodala proved his versatility by being the only rookie and 76er to record a triple-double during the 2004-05 NBA season, despite averaging 9 points and 5.7 rebounds per game. His efforts were rewarded when he was named to the All-Rookie First Team. His all around play earned him comparisons with all-time great Scottie Pippen, as well as to current NBA star and Arizona alumnus Richard Jefferson.

Iguodala was one of four players among qualifiers in 2006-07 to average at least 18 points, 5 rebounds and 5 assists (Kobe Bryant, LeBron James, and Tracy McGrady). Over his final 29 games played in 2006-07, he averaged 20.0 points, 6.7 assists and 6.1 rebounds per game. He's just the third player over the past 20 years to start at least the first 200 games of his career (Clarence Weatherspoon w/213 from 1992-1995 and Mike Bibby w/248 from 1999-2002). Also, he led the Philadelphia 76ers in scoring, minutes, free throws, and steals as a 3rd-year player, becoming the youngest player to do so since Allen Iverson in the 1999-2000 NBA season.

JUWAN HOWARD

Juwan Howard graduated from Chicago Vocational High in Chicago, while growing up in the projects on the city's South Side. Howard rode the El (elevated train) to school, had to practice in an unheated gym, and changed clothes for home games in a classroom. By the end of his senior year though, college recruiters rated him as the country's best high school center, and he earned Illinois High School Player of the Year.

Howard's career took an unusual turn during his freshman year at the University of Michigan. Michigan had a fine crop of five freshman recruits (Howard, Chris Webber, Jalen Rose, Jimmy King, and Ray Jackson) who all started by the time Michigan received their postseason invitation. Sportswriters dubbed them "The Fab Five." Michigan won its first five games and reached the championship game, but they lost handily in the National Championship game to Duke. The Fab Five remain a stunning success and Howard performed well enough to garner Honorable Mention Big-Ten honors.

After finishing his sophomore year second for the Wolverines in rebounding and third in scoring, Howard received still more recognition by earning Second Team Big-Ten and Honorable Mention All-American Nominations. Again the team reached the NCAA Championship game, but again it lost, although this time the game was closer. North Carolina won the title in the final seconds when Webber called a time-out the Wolverines did not have.

Webber left school for the NBA before Howard's junior season, leaving Howard and Jalen Rose as team leaders. Howard led Michigan in scoring and rebounding that season, and was named First Team All-Big Ten and Third Team All-America. Michigan didn't reach the Final Four that season, but when Howard left for the NBA, his stock had risen to make him one of the top college prospects in the country.

The Washington Bullets used the fifth selection in the 1994 NBA Draft to select Howard. Howard's rookie year removed any doubts about his potential. He finished second on the team in scoring and rebounding, and played in the Rookie All-Star Game at mid-season. That season Howard gained a unique distinction off the floor when he became the first player to leave college early and still earn his degree in four years.

Howard has always been regarded as a consistent hard working player. During his career, Howard has also been forced into being the first option; a role he was not particularly suited for. He became the Wizards' first option out of default after Chris Webber was traded. His level of play did not measure up to expectations and his status as a big time player was criticized by fans. A similar situation surfaced in two years with the Denver Nuggets as well. Howard was the first option and the Nuggets were among the worst teams in the West.

ANTOINE WALKER

Walker attended Mount Carmel High School, in Chicago, where he attained all-state status as a senior and earned a full scholarship to play for Rick Pitino at the University of Kentucky. He was a starting forward on the Wildcats' 1996 NCAA Men's Division I Basketball Championship winning team. As a freshman at Kentucky he was named SEC Tournament MVP. In his sophomore year Antoine was named All-SEC First, All-SEC Tournament and to the All-NCAA Regional Teams. After his sophomore season he declared for the 1996 NBA Draft and was picked sixth overall by the Boston Celtics.

Walker later teamed with Paul Pierce to help Boston reach the Eastern Conference finals in 2002, defeating the Philadelphia 76ers and Detroit Pistons before falling to the New Jersey Nets. Walker was selected to three NBA All-Star Game appearances, including the year when they reached the conference finals. He was voted onto the All-Star starting 5 by the fans that year.

Walker is a versatile big man who can play either forward spot. He is mostly used as a small forward, where he establishes himself as a prolific (career average 19.0 points per game) and deft rebounder, using his 6-foot-9 frame well (career average of 8.3 rebounds per game). He is also known as a capable passer, as 3.9 career assists per game proves. Walker is also known for his ability to shoot three-point field goals, as he has taken 3771 three-point attempts in his career (as of September 2006), averaging 5 per game, and made 1241 of them (.329). On August 2, 2005, Walker was involved in a 5-team, 13-player deal (the largest trade in NBA history) that sent him from the Celtics to the Miami Heat. On June 20, 2006, he won his first NBA Championship with the Miami Heat contributing 14 points and 11 rebounds in the final game of the series.

COREY MAGGETTE

He excelled at Fenwick High School in Oak Park, Illinois, where he was an All-American in basketball and also an Illinois high school state track finalist in long jump and triple jump. He was originally drafted with the 13th overall pick in the 1999 NBA Draft out of Duke University by the Seattle SuperSonics, but was immediately traded to the Orlando Magic. Along with teammate Elton Brand, Maggette is notable as one of the first Duke players to leave before the end of his athletic eligibility during the tenure of coach Mike Krzyzewski.

During his career with the Los Angeles Clippers, Maggette has established himself as a solid forward and developed into a perennial 20 per game scorer. Known for excellent jumping ability (he participated in the Slam Dunk Contest at the 2001 NBA All-star weekend) as well as his propensity to create contact and get to the free throw line. Maggette is consistently among the league leaders in free throws attempted and made. He experienced a banner year in 2004-05, touting career highs in points, rebounds, assists and free throw percentage while leading the Clippers to a 37-45 record, one of their best showings in years. During the

2008 off-season, Maggette signed a five year contract to play for the Golden State Warriors.

KEN NORMAN

Norman, nicknamed "Snake Norman" and "the snake" graduated from Crane High School in Chicago, Illinois. He played collegiately at the University of Illinois. He was selected 19th overall by the Los Angeles Clippers of the 1987 NBA Draft. Norman played for the Clippers, Milwaukee Bucks and Atlanta Hawks in 10 NBA seasons. His best year as a pro came during the 1988-89 season as a Clipper, when he averaged 18.1 points in 80 games. In his NBA career, Norman played in a total of 646 games and scored 8,717 points.

LAPHONSO ELLIS

He was an outstanding high school basketball player at East St. Louis Lincoln High School, where he led the Lincoln Tigers to two straight Illinois Class AA boys' basketball championships in 1987 and 1988. LaPhonso ended up attending the University of Notre Dame. Ellis' Notre Dame squad only qualified for the NCAA tournaments his freshman year.

Ellis was one of four captains of the 1991-92 Notre Dame team. Throughout his career, he scored 1,505 career points, averaged 15.5 points per game to earn school rankings of 12th and 22nd, respectively. He recorded 200 career blocks, a school record. He ranks third on the school's career rebounding list with 1,075, and eighth on the career rebounding list, with 11.1 rpg. He led the '91-92 team in scoring (17.7 ppg), rebounding (11.7 rpg), field goal percentage (.631) and blocked shots (2.6 bpg). He paced Notre Dame in blocked shots in each of his four seasons, the only player in school history to do so.

Ellis graduated from Notre Dame on time with a degree in accounting from the undergraduate college of business. He was the fifth overall selection in the 1992 NBA, picked by the Denver Nuggets, and was named to the 1992 All-Rookie first team. He subsequently played for Atlanta, Minnesota and Miami, where he retired after the 2003 season.

JOHNNY "RED" KERR

Although Jonny Kerr's first passion was soccer, an eight-inch growth spurt during his senior year at Tilden Technical High School compelled him to turn to basketball. The 6'9" center soon led his school's basketball team to the 1950 Chicago Public League Championship. After high school, he attended the University of Illinois, where he scored 1,299 points during his three years with the school's varsity team. The highlights of his collegiate career occurred in 1952, when he helped the Fighting Illini win the Big Ten Championship and advance to the NCAA Final four. he was the Big Ten Conference Most Valuable Player in 1954.

In 1954, the Syracuse Nationals selected Red Kerr with the sixth overall pick in the NBA Draft. During his first season (1954-55), Kerr averaged 10.5 points and 6.6 rebounds and helped the Nationals capture their first NBA Championship. He would go on to become a three time All-Star (1956, 1959, 1963) with the Nationals, despite playing in the shadow of future Hall of Famer Dolph Schayes.

In 1963, the Nationals relocated to Philadelphia, and became known as the 76ers. Two years later, Kerr was traded to the Baltimore Bullets for Wali Jones. After averaging 11.0 points and 8.3 rebounds during the 1965-1966 season, Kerr was selected by the Chicago Bulls in the 1965-66 NBA Expansion Draft. However, Kerr voluntarily retired so that he could become the coach of his hometown's new basketball team. He ended his career with respectable totals of 12,480 points and 10,092 rebounds, and he held the NBA record for most consecutive games played (844) until 1983 when he was surpassed by Randy Smith.

Kerr's Chicago Bulls went 33-48 in 1966-67 and became the first expansion team to win a playoff berth in its inaugural year. For this accomplish- ment, Kerr was rewarded the NBA Coach of the Year Award. The Bulls went 29-53 the following season, rallying from a 1-15 start to earn another playoff berth. However, feuds with team owner Dick Klein forced Kerr to leave the Bulls during the summer of 1968 and sign with the Phoenix Suns, another expansion team in need of its first coach. Unfortunately, the Suns finished with a 16-66 record in 1968-69, and after starting the 1969-70 season with a 15-23 record, Kerr was forced to resign. He now works as a broadcaster for the Chicago Bulls.

DARIUS MILES

Miles attended East St. Louis High School in East St. Louis, Illinois, and after failing to receive a qualifying SAT score to attend St. John's University, entered the 2000 NBA Draft. He was selected by the Los Angeles Clippers as the 3rd overall pick; at the time this was the highest that a player entering the NBA directly from high school had been drafted. He was the first player in NBA history drafted straight out of high school to receive All-Rookie honors. He also played for the Cleveland Cavaliers and more recently the Portland Trail Blazers.

During the 2004-05 season, Miles made headlines after a confrontation with then-coach Maurice Cheeks in which he reportedly insulted him with racial slurs and remarked that the didn't care if the team lost the next 20 games since Cheeks was going to be fired anyway. This led to his suspension for two games. Miles has been criticized for having tremendous talent, but a questionable work-ethic. He missed the entire 2006-07 NBA season due to a microfracture surgery. It also kept him out of action for the entire 2007-08 season. Finally, he was placed on waivers by Portland and was an unsigned free agent, until he signed with the Boston Celtics during the 2008 offseason. However, he was waived again prior to the start of the regular season.

BEN WILSON

Ben Wilson was more than a promising athlete. He had touched the hearts and minds of thousands of teenagers. Then he was dead, the victim of an assassin's bullet on the eve of the opening game of the 1984-85 season, eight months after he led Simeon to the state championship. He had gone from the last man on a sixteen-member frosh-soph squad to the top-rated prospect in the country.

Ben "Benji" Wilson was born in Chicago, Illinois and led Simeon Vocational High School (now known as Simeon Career Academy) to the school's first Illinois State boys' basketball championship in 1984. At 6-foot-7, Wilson was selected All-Tournament first team. Benji was the first in Chicago history to ever be named top high school player in the nation. His friend Nick Anderson wore the jersey number 25 during his career in his honor. His story was the focus of a 1977 Nike advertisement that aired during the NBA playoffs. Although dead, gunned down, Wilson would live on in the memory of his friends at Simeon.

JIM ARD

Born in Harvey, Illinois, Ard was an all-state basketball player at Thornton High School Ard led the Thornton to tho Illinois boys' basketball state championship in 1966, and was an All-Tournament Fist Team selection. A 6'8" forward/center, Ard attended the University of Cincinnati and played there collegiately. Afterwards, he was drafted in the first round (6th overall) by the Seattle SuperSonics in the 1970 NBA Draft.

Ard began his professional career in 1970 with the New York Nets of the American Basketball Association (ABA). He is best known for his three years (1974-77) with the National Basketball Association's Boston Celtics, for whom he provided rebounding and hustle-play as a backup for Dave Cowens. He also played briefly for the Chicago Bulls.

Ard sank the go-ahead free throws in game five of the 1976 NBA Finals, a triple-overtime game between the Celtics and the Phoenix Suns. Those free throws have been described as "the two most historic free throws in both Celtics and NBA history." The Celtics went on to win that series for the 1976 NBA Championship.

ARCHIE DEES

A 6'8' forward/center, Dees started his basketball career at Mount Carmel High School in Chicago, Illinois where he was named an All-American his senior year. Afterwards he attended Indiana University, where he received the Big Ten Conference Most Valuable Player award twice, 1957 and 1958. He is one of just four people (the others being Jerry Lucas, Cazzie Russell, and Scott May) to have received multiple Big Ten MVP honors. When he graduated in 1958, he was drafted in the 1st round (2nd overall) of the 1958 NBA Draft by the Cincinnati Royals, and he went on to play four seasons in the league with the Royals, Detroit

Pistons, Chicago Packers, and St. Louis Hawks. Dees was inducted into the Indiana University Hall of Fame in 1983. In 2001, he was named to the Indiana University All-Century Team. He currently lives in Bloomington, Indiana.

JIM BREWER

Born in Maywood, Illinois, Brewer was a basketball standout at Proviso East. In his senior year, Brewer was a 6'6" All-American premier post player known for his tenacious defense. He led Proviso East to the 1969 Illinois boys' basketball state championship. He averaged 16.5 points per game for four tournament games and was selected All-Tournament First Team.

Brewer attended the University of Minnesota before being drafted by the Cleveland Cavaliers in the 1st round (2nd pick overall) of the 1973 NBA Draft. He was the Big Ten Conference Most Valuable Player in 1972. He played nine seasons in the NBA before retiring in 1982. He played on the 1972 Men's Olympic basketball team that won the Silver Medal in Munich, Germany. He also was a member of the Los Angeles Lakers 1981-82 NBA championship team. He worked as a director of player personnel, assistant coach and assistant to the general manager for the Minnesota Timberwolves (1990-94), an assistant coach for the Los Angeles Clippers (1994-98) and an assistant coach with the Toronto Raptors (2000-02).

STEVE KUBERSKI

Kuberski played high school basketball at Moline High School, where he led the Maroons to the Elite Eight in the 1965 season. Favored Moline lost to Chicago Marshall 75-72, and Collinsville went on to win the the state title. As a senior, Kuberski averaged 28 points per game and was included on a list of the top 30 players in the country with Lew Alcindor (later Kareem Adbul-Jabbar). UCLA recruited him, but he chose Illinois. However, after two years, he transferred to Bradley after being implicated in the slush fund scandal that devastated Illinois football and basketball programs and resulted in the firing of coaches Pete Elliott and Harry Combes. He averaged 24 points as a junior, and then declared for the NBA.

Kuberski played nine NBA seasons for the Boston Celtics, Milwaukee Bucks, and Buffalo Braves averaging 3.8 rebounds and 5.5 points per game. Kuberski won two NBA titles with the Celtics in 1973-74 and 1975-76. His greatest claim to fame though, is being the last Celtic to wear number 33 before Larry Bird. Kuberski now owns a company in the New England area, making lockers for schools and warehouse products.

MARCUS LIBERTY

In 1986, when he was beginning his senior year at Martin Luther King Jr. High School in Chicago, Marcus Liberty was one of seven sixth-through 12th-grade basketball players profiled in *Sports Illustrated.* All ranked among the top prospects in the nation at the time. 1n 1986, Liberty led King to a 32-1 record and the Class AA championship. In 1987, Liberty was Illinois Mr. Basketball and led King to second place in the state tournament, setting Class AA records with 143 points in four games and 41 points in the championship game.

Few players could matchup to Liberty's talent and flair for the game. He grew up on the West Side and idolized such players as Bo Ellis, Sonny Parker, Rickey Green, Isiah Thomas, and Ben Wilson. As a freshman, he led Crane to the Public League's frosh-soph title. Then he transferred to King. Later, he attended college at the University of Illinois, where he averaged 17.8 points as a junior. He then decided to leave and make himself eligible for the NBA draft. Perhaps he would have been a lottery pick had he stayed for his senior year.

He was selected by the Denver Nuggets in the 2nd round (42nd overall) of the 1990 NBA Draft. Liberty played for the Nuggets and Detroit Pistons in 4 NBA seasons. His best season as a pro was during the 1991-92 NBA season when he appeared in 75 games for the Nuggets, averaging 9.3 points per game.

BILL ROBINZINE

A 6-foot-7 Chicago native, Robinzine attended Phillips High School in Chicago. Afterward, he attended DePaul University in Chicago and was drafted by the Kansas City Kings with the 10th pick (10th overall) in the 1st round of the 1975 NBA Draft. He played five seasons for the Kansas City Kings. He also played for Cleveland, Dallas, and Utah.

Robinzine played no high school basketball but sufficiently for coach Ray Meyer to earn a spot on DePaul's freshman team and a starting position as a sophomore. Robinzine was not an All-American, but his stellar play in a postseason college all-star game in which he was invited to play only because another player dropped out, helped to make him the Kings' first draft choice. He became a starter in his second season. He was injured midway in the 1979-80 season, and he was traded to the Cleveland Cavaliers the following year and to the Dallas Mavericks less than a month later. His last season with the Jazz, he played sparingly.

Friends insist that Robinzine did not drink, gamble or use drugs. Robinzine's 1981 salary was about $200,000. If he were offered a contract for the 1982 season, it might have meant a cut in pay for playing a substitute's role. Robinzine had rejected a chance to play in Europe. He was experiencing some financial problems, but they were manageable. Then his father found him slumped behind the wheel of his Oldsmobile Toronado that he had parked in a Kansas City garage. The police ruled his death a suicide caused by carbon-monoxide asphyxiation. Robinzine was 29 years old. Robinzine's death came perhaps not at the end of a reasonably successful career, in which he was averaging more than 10 points and six rebounds a game for seven seasons.

KEVIN GAMBLE

A Springfield, Illnois native, a 6-6 all-state senior Kevin Gamble as well as 6-8 sophomore Ed Horton, Illinois Mr. Basketball 1985, led Springfield Lanphier to their first Illinois state boys' basketball championship. He and Horton combined to make 15 of 19 shots in the title game, including a crucial three-point play by Gamble, for a 57-53 win over Peoria Central. Kevin Gamble made the All-Tournament First Team that year, 1983.

He attended Lincoln College, Illinois and the University of Iowa before being selected with the 17th pick of the 3rd round (63rd overall) by the Portland Trail Blazers in the 1987 NBA Draft. He played with the Blazers, the Boston Celtics, Miami Heat and Sacramento Kings, and also in the Continental Basketball Association. He retired from professional basketball in 1997.

Gamble played seven seasons with the Celtics from 1988 through 1994, averaging double averaging four of those seasons. For three consecutive seasons, from 1990-1993, Gamble played in all 82 games. He was a pure professional who came to play every night.

Gamble became the men's basketball coach at the University of Illinois at Springfield in the American Midwest Conference (NAIA). Gamble is the first head coach in the college's history as they had just started up their basketball program. Since 2004 he has been involved in the real estate industry.

ED HORTON

Along with Gamble, as a 6-foot-8 sophomore Horton led Springfield Lanphier to its first Illinois boys' state basketball championship in 1983. He led Springfield Lanphier to runner-up in the Illinois 1985 Class AA state championship and earned Illinois Mr. Basketball that year. He played collegiately at the university of Iowa. He was selected by the Washington Bullets in the 2nd round (39th overall) of the 1989 NBA Draft. Horton played just one year in the NBA, appearing in 45 games and averaging 4.5 ppg for the Bullets during the 1989-90 season.

EDDIE JOHNSON

Eddie Johnson was born in Chicago, Illinois and attended Westinghouse High School on the city's West Side. A sharpshooting 6'7" forward/guard, Johnson attended the University of Illinois before being selected by the Kansas City Kings with the 29th pick overall in the 2nd round of the 1981 NBA Draft. Johnson would play for the Kings, the Phoenix Suns, the Seattle SuperSonics, the Charlotte Hornets, the Indiana Pacers, and the Houston Rockets of the NBA. He spent 17 seasons in the NBA. Although his 19,202 points was the 22nd highest total in NBA history at the time of his retirement, Johnson was never selected to play in the All-Star game nor even chosen for an All-NBA team. In fact, the "awards highlight" of his career occurred in 1989, when he received the NBA Sixth Man of the Year Award as a member of the Suns.

Along with the Sixth Man of the Year Award, he was also remembered for hitting the game-winning three-pointer as time expired in a 95-92 Rockets win over the Utah Jazz in Game 4 of the 1997 Western Conference Finals. After his playing career was over, Johnson turned to broadcasting, serving as color commentator for the Arizona State University men's basketball team, the WNBA's Phoenix Mercury, and currently the Phoenix Suns.

ROGER POWELL

He attended Joliet High School in Joliet, Illinois, graduating in 2001. Powell played the forward position in high school and in college. He played colegiately at the University of Illinois. He graduated fro the University of Illinois with a degree in Speech Communications. Powell's father was a former Joliet Central High School and Illinois State player.

Powell was a three-year starter and a four-year letter winner for Joliet High School. As a junior, he led the Steelmen to a 20-8 record, averaging 19 points and eight rebounds. Powell helped his squad win the SICA West Conference as a junior and senior. Also as a junior, he earned a bronze medal as a member of the 1999 USA Basketball Men's Youth Development Festival North Team. Powell also made the Pontiac Holiday Tourny all-Tournament Team and was second team all-state.

As a senior, Powell averaged 20.7 points and 9 rebounds for a 25-5 sectional finalist that was ranked No.3 in the Chicago area. He earned First Team all-state honors at Joliet in 2001 from the *Chicago Tribune, Chicago Sun-Times, The Champaign-Urbana News Gazette,* Associated Press and Illinois Basketball Coaches Association. He was considered a consensus Top 100 prospect in the nation and was fourth in voting for Illinois Mr. Basketball. He played in the Wendy's All-Star Classic and earned MVP honors at the IBCA All-Star Game following his senior year.

At the University of Illinois, he scored his 1,000th point vs. Indiana on Feb. 6, 2005 and ended his career ranked 26th on the Illini all-time scoring list with 1,178 career points. He also ranks fifth in school history in career field goal percentage at 57.2 percent (456-797). Powell then participated in various NBA summer leagues looking to be picked up by an NBA roster. He eventually made the Seattle SuperSonics' training roster roster but failed to make the final roster. Powell continued to pursue a career in the NBA trying out for the Utah Jazz where he was reunited with former Illini teammates Dee Brown and Deron Williams. After working relentlessly over the summer, Powell made the Utah Jazz final roster for the 2006-07 NBA season. However, he was cut in mid January. He's currently playing for the Arkansas Rimrockers of the NBDL. Although, with the 2008-09 NBA season approaching, the Chicago Bulls added him to the training camp roster.

ANDRE BROWN

Brown played competitively at Leo High School and DePaul University; both in Chicago. Brown was a member of the Atlanta Hawks for almost a month, but prior to the 2006-07 NBA season, he was cut from the training camp roster. Brown was selected with the second overall pick in the 2006 NBA D-League draft by the Sioux Falls Skyforce and was named D-League Performer of the Week for December 18, 2006 after averaging 23.3 points and 11.2 rebounds in 13 games during the month. He led the league in scoring with 22.8 points per game, and was second in rebounding at 10.8 rebounds per game.

He played for the San Antonio Spurs during the Rocky Mountain Revue in Salt Lake City, and was top scorer for the team with 13 points in the fourth game. During 2005 and 2006, Brown played professionally in Seoul, South Korea for the Daegu Orions of the Korean Basketball League. He was signed to a 10-day contract by the Seattle SuperSonics on January 5, 2007. After averaging 4.0 points and 2.0 rebounds in four games, he was signed to a second 10-day contract on January 15. He was subsequently signed for the rest of the season on January 25 after playing seven games, averaging 5.0 points and 2.9 rebounds. In 38 total games for the Sonics in 2006-07 he averaged 2.4 points and 1.9 rebounds per game. A power forward-center, he played the 2007-08 NBA season for the Memphis Grizzlies of the NBA, with whom he signed after spending his first season with the Seattle SuperSonics. On September 27, 2008 the Charlotte Bobcats signed the free agent forward-center to contract.

BOBBY SIMMONS

Simmons currently plays professional basketball for the New Jersey Nets of the National Basketball Association. He was traded from the Milwaukee Bucks during the 2007-08 offseason. Simmons played three years of college basketball at DePaul University. Simmons was selected in the second round (42nd oversll) of the 2001 NBA Draft by the Seattle SuperSonics. The 6'6", 228 lb small forward from Simeon Vocational High School (now Simeon Academy High School) had a breakout year during the 2004-05 NBA season with the Los Angeles Clippers in which he averaged a career-high 16.4 points per game. He was rewarded for his stellar play with the NBA Most Improved Player Award. However, since his breakout year with the Clippers, Simmons has struggled to reach the same level of play. In his first year with the Bucks, his points, rebounds and shooting percentages all declined. Then in 2006, an ankle injury forced him to miss the entire 2006-07 season. For his career, Simmons has averaged 10.7 points, 4.3 rebounds. 1.9 assists and 1.0 steals per game.

BOB LACKEY

Lackey a 6'6" forward attended Evanston High School in Evanston, Illinois and led Evanston High to an Illinois state title in 1968. He played collegiately for

Casper Junior College in Wyoming for two years. Lackey lettered at Marquette University during the 1970-71 and 1971-72 seasons after transferring from junior college. In his senior season, he led the Warriors to a 25-4 record and claimed All-American honors from the Helms Athletic Foundation.

Lackey was drafted by the National Basketball Association Atlanta Hawks and the New York Nets of the old American Basketball Association. Lackey signed with the Nets, played a full season and averaged 5.9 points per game. In his second season, he played three games before the Nets cut him. Lackey headed for Europe, where he played in the Netherlands and in France. After his European stint, Lackey had a tryout with the Milwaukee Bucks but wasn't signed. He died in June, 2002 at 53 of cancer in Evanston.

KEVIN GARNETT

In his first three high school years, Garnett played for Mauldin High School in South Carolina. However, during the summer prior to his senior year of high school, Kevin was in the general vicinity of a fight between black and white students. Although not directly involved, Garnett was arrested. Due to the racially charged incident and fearful of being a target, Garnett decided to leave Mauldin. He transferred to Farragut Career Academy in Chicago, Illinois for his senior year of high school. He led Farragut to a 28-2 record and was named National High School Player of the Year by *USA Today*. He was named Mr. Basketbll of State of Illinois after averaging 25.2 points, 17.9 rebounds, 6.7 assists and 6.5 blocks while shooting 66.7% from the field. In four years of high school, Garnett posted an impressive 2,533 points, 1,807 rebounds and 739 blocked shots. He was named the Most Outstanding Player at the McDonald's All-American Game after registering 18 points, 11 rebounds, 4 assists and 3 blocked shots. He then declared himself eligible for the 1995 NBA Draft.

After graduating from Farragut Career Academy, he was the fifth player drafted in 1995. He became the first NBA player drafted directly out of high school in 20 years. His nicknames include "The Big Ticket," "KG," "The Kid," and formerly "The Franchise" (due to leaving the Minnesota Timberwolves after being known as their franchise player). The 6'11" 220lb power forward is regarded as one of the best all around players in the game today. His accomplishments include having been voted Most Valuable Player of the 2003-04 NBA season, 2003 NBA All-Star Game MVP, being named to 11 All-Star teams, and being named to nine All-NBA and All-Defensive teams. Also, he was named the 2008 NBA Defensive Player of the Year. He led the Boston Celtics in scoring and rebounding in the 2008 playoffs, as the Boston Celtics claimed their 17th NBA championship.

He is the first player in NBA history to:
• average at least 20 points, 10 rebounds, and 5 assists per game for 6 consecutive seasons. (1999-2005)
• average at least 20 points, 10 rebounds, and 4 assists per game for 9 consecutive seasons. (1998-2007)

- reach at least 18,000 points, 10,000 rebounds, 4,000 asissts, 1,200 steals, and 1,500 blocks in a playing career.
- to be traded for a total of 7 players. (from the Minnesota Timberwolves to the Boston Celtics for Ryan Gomes, Gerald Green, Al Jefferson, Theo Ratliff, Sebastian Telfair and two 1st round draft choices on July 31, 2007).
- He also became the youngest player in NBA history to play in 1,000 regular season games.

TYRONE NESBY

Tyrone Nesby was born in Cairo, Illinois and was a standout basketball at Cairo High School. Undrafted from the University of Neveda, Las Vegas and Vincennes University, he played for the Los Angeles Clippers from 1998-2000, and with the Washington Wizards from 2000-2002. In Europe he played with the Olympia Larissa BC (Greece) (2002-03), Pallacanestro Varese (Italy) (2003-04), FMP Zoleznik (Serbia) (2004), and BC Lietuvos Rytas (Lithuania) (2004-05). In 2006-07, he played with the ABA's Las Vegas Venom. The 6'6" forward-guard averaged 9.5 points per game for his NBA career, and had a career high 30 points against Seattle (5/5/99).

KEON CLARK

Arian Keon Clark was born in Danville, Illinois and starred at Danville High School. After a collegiate career at two different junior colleges and UNLV, Clark was selected 13th overall by the Orlando Magic in the 1998 NBA Draft but was traded to the Denver Nuggets. He began his professional career with Denver where he enjoyed a stable first three years in the NBA, improving steadily.

A 6'11" center-forward, Clark would go on to play for the Toronto Raptors, Sacramento Kings, and Utah Jazz. With the Jazz, he only played two games before being traded to the Phoenix Suns for whom he never played. His off-court issues ultimately led to his release from the Suns and exile from the league. During his stay in the league, Clark was known for his excellent jumping ability and his unusually skinny legs. In 2002, Clark posted averages of 11.3 points and 1.51 blocks per game, while also finishing ninth in the NBA in total personal fouls.

SHERELL FORD

While at Proviso East High School in Maywood, Illinois, Ford was a teammate of fellow NBA player Michael Finley, and Donnie Boyce. They combined to lead the Pirates to the first of back-to-back Illinois state AA titles, where Ford was a First Team All-Tournament selection in 1991, along with Finley. A 6'7" forward from the University of Illinois at Chicago, Ford played in 1 NBA season in 1995 with the Sonics. He was selected by the Seattle SuperSonics in the 1st round (26th overall) of the 1995 NBA Draft.

SHELLIE MCMILLON

McMillon starred on the legendary 1954 DuSable Panthers basketball team that finished second in the Illinois state tournament, along witn All-American guard Paxton Lumpkin and all-state sharpshooter "Sweet" Charlie Brown. He played collegiately at Bradley University, where he had a stellar career. He was drafted by the Detroit Pistons in the 6th round (3rd pick, 42nd overall) of the 1958 NBA Draft. He played in the NBA 4 seasons with Detroit and St. Louis. A 6'5" 205 lb forward, McMillon is remembered for grabbing a loose ball with seconds to play and sinking his shot. He was fouled in the process and sank the free throw to give Bradley the N.I.T. title 84-83 over the Memphis Tigers at Madison Square Garden.

KENNY BATTLE

Kenny Battle was born in Aurora, Illinois and was a standout high school basketball player at West Aurora High School. Battle played collegiately at the University of Illinois. He was selected by the Detroit Pistons in the 1st round (27th overall) of the 1989 NBA Draft. He was then traded on draft day to the Phoenix Suns along with Michael Williams in exchange for the Suns' first round draft choice (24th overall), Anthony Cook. Battle played 4 NBA seasons for the Phoenix Suns, Denver Nuggets, Boston Celtics and Golden State Warriors. His best year as a pro came during the 1991-92 NBA season when he split time with the Suns and Nuggets, appearing in 56 games and averaging 6.7 ppg. Prior to that, he competed in the NBA's 1990 slam dunk contest.

NORM COOK

A 6'8" forward, Cook was born in Chicago, Illinois and starred in high school at Lincoln in Lincoln, Illinois. He played collegiately at Kansas University. He holds a KU record for the most points in a freshman debut with 21 against Murray State (12-1-73). He was drafted by the Boston Celtics in the 1st round (16th pick, 16th overall) of the 1976 NBA Draft. He played in the NBA for 2 seasons with the Boston Celtics (1976-77) and the Denver Nuggets (1977-78). He played a total of 27 games and scored a total of 65 points. He eventually went into coaching and has coached basketball collegiately.

BRIAN COOK

The son of Norm, he led his high school team, the Lincoln Community High School Railsplitters, to the quarterfinals of the Illinois High School Association class AA state boys basketball tournament. Cook played 4 years at the University of Illinois, beginning with the 1999-2000 season. He was co Big Ten Freshman of the Year during his first year at Illinois. As a senior in the 2002-03 season, Cook led the Fighting Illini in scoring with 20.0 points per game, and received the *Chicago Tribune* Silver Basketball as the Most Valuable Player of the Big Ten Conference.

That same season, Cook was named Second-Team All-American by *The Sporting News* and Third-Team All-American by the Associated Press, the National Association of Basketball Coaches, and *The Basketball Times,* as well as Big Ten Player of the Year and First-Team Big Ten by the coaches and the media. Cook left Illinois as the school's third all-time leading scorer with 1,748 total points, an average of 13.2 points per game.

Cook was drafted out of the University of Illinois with the 24th pick of the first round of the 2003 NBA Draft by the Los Angeles Lakers. As a professional, Cook has become a player who predominantly shoots from the perimeter, away from the basket. He's currently a reserve power forward with the Orlando Magic after being traded to them by the Lakers.

ALANDO TUCKER

Alando was born in Lockport, Illinois and attended Lockport Township High School in his native Lockport. Tucker averaged 21.6 points and seven rebounds per game as a junior. He was one of only two juniors to be named to the *Herald News* AA all-area team. As a senior he earned all-state honors averaging 22.2 points while hauling in 7.7 rebounds and dishing 5.7 assists per game. Alando scored 35 points against the number one ranked team in the state, Joliet.

Tucker started off his college basketball career in 2002-03 starting 27 pf 32 games as a freshman. He averaged 12.0 points and 55.9 rebounds per game. In 2003-04, tucker played in only four games due to a right ankle injury. After the season he received a medical redshirt, which allowed him an additional year of eligibility. During 2004-05 season, Tucker started 30 of 31 games, and led the Badgers in scoring with 15.2 points. He also averaged 6.1 rebounds and 1.7 assists. The 2005-06 season saw Tucker average 19.0 points, 5.7 rebounds and 1.7 assists.

At the end of the 2006-07, Tucker was First-Team All-American in two polls (National Association of Basketball Coaches and Sporting News), while averaging 19.9 points, 5.4 rebounds and 2.0 assists his senior year. On March 10, 2007, Tucker broke the all-time Wisconsin scoring record (2,147 points) previously held by Michael Finley. He's primarily a small forward and is listed at 6-6, 205 lbs. Tucker was taken with the 29th pick in in the 2007 NBA Draft by the Phoenix Suns. He's still with the Suns organization, although he actually didn't perform exceptionally well his rookie season in Phoenix.

C.J. KUPEC

C.J. Kupec was born in Oak Lawn, Illinois and was a standout basketball player at Oak Lawn Community High School. He played collegiately at the University of Michigan. He was selected with the 2nd pick in the 4th round (40th overall) by the Los Angeles Lakers in the 1975 NBA Draft. The 6'8" forward played for the Los Angeles Lakers and the Houston Rockets during the 1970s, and Italy in the 1980s.

CUONZO MARTIN

Cuonzo Martin was born in East St. Louis, Illinois and was a standout basketball player Lincoln High School in East St. Louis. A 6'5" guard-forward at Purdue University, he helped the Boilermakers win consecutive back-to-back Big Ten titles in the mid-ninetees, along with NBA star Glenn Robinson. Known for his tough defense, he held future NBA players Shawn Respert of Michigan State and Wisconsin's Michael Finley to their season lows in scoring his senior year. Also, he held Purdue's career three-point field goal record (now held by Jaraan Cornell and second to David Teague).

Martin was the 57th pick in the 2nd round of the 1995 NBA Draft to the Atlanta Hawks. He played only seven career NBA games for the Vancouver Grizzlies (1995-96, an expansion team) and Milwaukee Bucks (1996-97). He also played professionally in the CBA and in Italy with Lin Serie A2 in 1997 for 4 months and for Cirio Avellino. Later, he was an associate head coach at Purdue University, under his former teammate, Matt Painter. He was previously assistant to his former coach, Gene Keady. Currently, he's the head basketball coach at Missouri State University in the Missouri Valley Conference.

ERIC ANDERSON

Eric Anderson was born in Chicago, Illinois. He attended St. Francis de Sales on Chicago's far southeast side and was named 1988's Mr. Basketball for the state of Illinois. After a college career at Indiana University, the 6'9" forward, who was not selected in the 1992 NBA Draft, signed with the New York Knicks for the 1992-93 NBA season, in which he played 16 games. He also played 11 games the following season before being waived. He holds NBA career averages of 1.6 points and 1.1 rebounds per game, and was an all-time 2-for-2 from the three-point line. He last saw action with the CBA's Fort Wayne Fury in 1998. He was, until 2007, the Athletic Director for Saint Theodore Guerin Catholic High School in Noblesville, Indiana.

SEAN LAMPLEY

Sean Lampley was born in Harvey, Illinois and attended St. Francis de Sales in Chicago. Lampley played small forward at the University of California, leading the Golden Bears to victory over Clemson in the 1999 National Invitation Tournament while earning MVP honors. In 2001, he led the team to the NCAA Tournament, but the Bears lost in the first round to Fresno State. Lampley ended his career as the only player in school history to rank in the top 10 in points (1,776, 1st), rebounds (889, 4th) and assists (295, 10th). He was named Pac-10 Player of the Year and Honorable Mention All-America his senior year by the AP.

Lampley was selected by the Chicago Bulls in the 2nd round (45th pick) of the 2001 NBA Draft. Although he never wore a Bulls uniform, Lampley played 35 games for the Miami Heat during the 2002-03 season and 10 games for the Golden State Warriors during the 2003-04 season. He competed with the Sacramento Kings in 2006 summer league play. On July 12, 2007, it was announced that Lampley was close to signing with the Australian NBL's Melbourne Tigers for the upcoming 2007-08 season.

MICKEY JOHNSON

Mickey was born in Chicago, Illinois and attended Lindblom High School on the South Side of the city. A 6'10" forward-center from tiny Aurora College, he was selected by the Portland Trail Blazers in the fourth round of the 1974 NBA Draft. The Blazers immediately traded Johnson to the Chicago Bulls, with whom he averaged just 3.8 points per game as a rookie. Johnson quickly improved, however, and moved into the Bulls' starting lineup during the middle of his second season.

A versatile scorer and aggressive rebounder, he averaged 17.3 points and 10.2 rebounds in 1976-77. The following season, he averaged 18.3 points and 9.1 rebounds. In 1979, he signed as a free agent with the Indiana Pacers, and averaged a career-high 19.1 points during his first and only season with them. He alson played for the Milwaukee Bucks, New Jersey Nets, and Golden State Warriors. He retired in 1986 with 12,748 career points and 6,465 career rebounds. He is the head coach of men's basketball at Malcolm X College in Chicago.

DEON THOMAS

Deon Thomas was born in Chicago, Illinois and was a standout basketball player at Simeon Vocational on the city's South Side. The 6'9' power forward played college basketball at the University of Illinios. Thomas finished his career as the all-time leading scorer in Fighting Illini history, 2129 career points and an 18.0 points per game scoring average. Thomas is the only men's basketball player in Illinois history to score at least 2,000 career points.

Prior to playing basketball at Illinois, Thomas was a central figure in a recruiting scandal. Regarded as one of the top prospects in high school basketball, Thomas was recruited by, among others, Illinois and the University of Iowa. An assistant coach at Iowa, Bruce Pearl, recorded a phone conversation with Thomas during which Thomas allegedly admitted to have been offered a Chevy Blazer and cash from Illinois. Pearl later turned the recording in to the NCAA, accompanied by a memo describing the event.

The NCAA charged Illinois with a major infraction on November 7, 1990. The NCAA cited Illinois with a "lack of institutional control" and implemented several recruiting restrictions and a one year postseason ban, since it was Illinois' third major violation in six years. Although those allegations by Pearl were never proven, Deon Thomas became a symbol of the intense rivalry between the universities of Illinois and Iowa. His recruitment and resulting NCAA investigation and punishment is naturally interpreted differently by many many Illinois supporters and many Iowa supporters, and the incident remains a catalyst for the heightened rivalry between Iowa and Illinois, years after his college career ended.

Thomas was selected by the Dallas Mavericks with the 28th selection of the 1994 NBA Draft, which was the first pick of the second round. Thomas never played in the NBA, having opted to play professional basketball in Europe and Israel. As of November 2006, Deon Thomas plays for PBC CSKA Sofia in Bulgaria. On November 13, 2006, in an interview for Bulgarian newspaper *Tema Sport* and Bulgarian television "Channel 3", Deon Thomas denied any wrong doing and swore that he didn't receive anything from the University of Illinois. In 2006, when asked in an interview about forgiving Pearl, Thomas said "it's hard to forgive a snake".

CHAPTER EIGHT

GREAT CENTERS

DAN ISSEL

Dan Issel was born in Batavia, Illinois and played basketball locally at Batavia High School. Issel played college basketball at the University of Kentucky under legendary coach Adolph Rupp. Issel was at UK 1996-70 and scored 2,138 points (an average of 25.7 per game) while being named an All-American for two of his three seasons there. (Freshman were not eligible to play varsity at the time). On February 7, 1970, Issel scored 53 points in a 120-85 victory over Mississippi, breaking Cliff Hagan's single-game record of 51.

Upon Issel's graduation in 1970, he signed to play for the Kentucky Colonels of the American Basketball Association (ABA). In his first season, Issel led the ABA in scoring with a scoring average of 29.9 points per game, and pulled down 13.2 rebounds per game. He was named the ABA Rookie of the Year in 1971, and was selected to the All-ABA Second Team. The following season, Issel raised his scoring average to 30.6 points per game, made the All-ABA First Team, and was named MVP of the 1972 ABA All-Star Game.

In 1975, Issel won an ABA title with the Colonels, who also featured sharp-shooting guard (and fellow ex-Kentucky Wildcat) Louie Dampier, as well as 7-2 center Artis Gilmore. After the Colonel's championship season Issel was sold by the Colonel's owners to the short-lived Baltimore Claws franchise and ended up with the Denver Nuggets following the ABA's merger with the NBA in 1976, and represented Denver in the 1977 NBA All-Star Game. He continued playing through the 1984-85 season, and received the NBA's J. Walter Kennedy Citizenship Award in 1985 for his outstanding service to the community. Issel accumulated over 27,000 points in his combined ABA and NBA career. At the time of his retirement, the only professional basketball players to have scored more points than Issel were Kareem Abdul Jabbar, Wilt Chamberlain and Julius Erving.

After he had been retired for awhile, he returned to the Nuggets as head coach in 1992 and led them to the playoffs. That year, the Nuggets pulled off the biggest upset to date in NBA history, knocking off the Seattle SuperSonics in five games. He retired three games into the 1995-96 season after facing criticism for his coaching style, saying he didn't like the person he'd become. He returned in 1998 as president and general manager, naming himself head coach again in December 1999, yielding his general manager's title to Kiki Vandeweghe. His second tenure was far less successful as the Nuggets failed to post a winning season.

His tenure ended on a rather sour note in December 2001. On Decemeber 10, after a close loss to the Charlotte Hornets, Issel heard a fan taunting him as he walked off the court at the Pepsi Center. Issel screamed, *"Hey, go drink another beer. Go drink another beer, you fucking Mexican piece of shit."* The incident was captured on Denver's NBC affiliate, KUSA-TV. He finally decided to resign on December 26, though some reports circulated that he'd been fired. Nevertheless, in 2003 he was elected into the Naismith Memorial Basketball Hall of Fame as a player

EDDY CURRY

Prior to becoming considered one of the best high school basketball players in the nation as a senior at Thornwood High School in South Holland, Illinois, Curry aspired to be a gymnast and did not pick up basketball until the 7th grade when he reluctingly went out for the school team. In 2001, Curry led his team to second place in the IHSA State Playoffs. Curry is one of three current professional athletes who call Thornwood their alma mater, the others being St. Louis Cardinals pitcher Mark Mulder, and Tampa Bay Rays designated hitter Cliff Floyd.

Curry was a *USA Today* First Team All-American, and was named *PARADE Magazine* High School Player of the Year. Curry was the MVP of the McDonald's All-American game scoring 28 points with 8 rebounds and 4 blocks in leading the West to a 131-125 victory. He led Thornwood High School to the Illinois State Championship game averaging 22.0 points, 9.0 rebounds and 6.0 blocked shots, shooting .640 from the field including 25.0 points and 10.0 rebounds in the state tournament. He averaged 24.6 points and 11.2 rebounds along with 4.8 blocks, as a junior.

Curry had signed a letter of intent to play at DePaul University but declared himself eligible for the 2001 NBA Draft in which the Chicago Bulls made him the fourth overall pick. Curry's contributions was limited as a rookie due to limited minutes. Curry improved his second season, leading the NBA in field goal percentage (58.5%) and becoming the first Bull to led the league in a major statistical category since Michael Jordan in 1998. His 2002-03 season was widely considered a disappointment as he failed to live up to expectations. In the 2004-05 season the Bulls improved by 28 wins and made the playoffs as the 22-year old Curry led the team in scoring before being hospitalized with an irregular heartbeat.

Curry was traded th the New York Knicks. Curry's inability to defend and rebound was a source of frustration for former coaches Scott Skiles and Larry Brown. The 2006-07 season seen a resurgence in Curry's performance under new coach Isiah Thomas, with Curry anointed the team's primary offensive option, averaging career highs in points (19.6), rebounds (7.1), and minutes (34.9) per game. On April 7, 2007 Curry scored a career best 43 points in an overtime win over the Milwaukee Bucks.

Nathaniel "Sweetwater" Clifton

A player who spent some years in all-black leagues before coming to the NBA, Clifton avoided divulging his age. He is reported to have been born in England, Arkansas, on October 13, 1922. Clifton's family moved to Chicago when he was eight. His birth name was Clifton Nathaniel, but after he became a high school star in Chicago he reversed the two names when sportswriters complained that the last name Nathaniel was too long to fit the headline. Standing over 6-foot-7 inches tall and weighing 235 pounds, Clifton dominated his opponents while playing on the basketball team at Chicago's DuSable High School. His hands spanned ten inches, and he could palm a basketball as easily as others might handle a tennis ball. In the city championship semifinals in his senior year in 1942, he scored 45 points, blowing away the former tournament record of 24. The *Chicago Daily News* called him one of the two greatest high school basketball players in Illinois history.

Clifton played one season at Xavier University in New Orleans before being drafted in the U.S. Army in 1944. He served three years in Europe and then turned professional on his return home, becoming the first black player to join the Dayton Metropolitans and then playing for the all-black New York Rens. In 1948 Clifton signed with the Harlem Globetrotters, the legendary African American masters of razzle-dazzle basketball. Clifton was signed for a reported annual salary of $10.000, which was said to be the highest salary paid to a black basketball player up to that time.

In the summer of 1950, after the Boston Celtics had drafted Chuck Cooper and officially broken the NBA's color line, Abe Saperstein sold Clifton's contract to the New York Knickerbockers for $12,500, of which Clifton pocketed $2,500. He remained on good terms with Saperstein to continue to play for the Globetrotters during the NBA off-season. Clifton made his Knicks debut on November 3, 1950 and quickly became an integral part of the newly powerful squad. Playing at forward he was assigned to guard opposing centers. The Knicks made the NBA finals during each of Clifton's first three years. His career with the Knicks was a solid one. His best year with the Knicks was the 1956-57 season, when he averaged 13 points per game and played in the NBA All-Star Game. After that he was traded to the Detroit Pistons and, after his first year there, in which he was frustrated with his lack of playing time, he left the NBA.

Immensely popular in Chicago, Clifton had continued to live in his neighborhood. With no pension coming from the NBA and married, he had to find a job. He settled on driving a taxi and continued to do so for the rest of his life. Inducted into the Black Athletes Hall of Fame in 1978, Clifton died at the wheel of his cab near Chicago's Union Station on August 31, 1990.

George Mikan

George Mikan was born in Joliet, Illinois to Croatian parents with roots in Vivodina near Karlovac. As a boy, he shattered his knee so badly that he was kept in bed for a year and a half. In 1938, Mikan attended the Chicago Archbishop Quigley Preparatory Seminary and originally wanted to be a priest, but then moved back home to finish at Joliet Catholic. Mikan did not seem destined to become an athlete. When Mikan entered Chicago's DePaul University in 1942, he was 6'10" tall and weighed 245 pounds. He moved awkwardly because of his frame, and needed thick glasses for his near-sightedness. Mikan's only early sports interest had been the game of marbles, in which he won a countywide marbles-shooting championship.

Mikan met 28-year-old rookie DePaul basketball coach Ray Meyer, who saw potential in the bright and intelligent, but also clumsy and shy freshman. Meyer's thoughts were revolutionary, because back then, common sense dictated that tall players were too awkward to ever play basketball well. In the following months, Meyer transformed Mikan into a confident, aggressive player who took pride in his height rather than being ashamed of it. Meyer and Mikan worked out intensely, and Mikan learned how to make hook shots accurately with either hand. This routine would become known as the *Mikan Drill.* In addition, Meyer made Mikan punch a speed bag, take dancing lessons and jump rope to make him a complete athlete.

From his first NCAA college games for DePaul on, Mikan dominated his peers. He intimidated opponents with his size and strength, was unstoppable on offense with his hook shot, and soon established a reputation as one of the hardest grittiest players in the league. He often played through injuries and punished opposing centers with hard fouls. In addition, Mikan also stunned the basketball world by his unique ability to goaltend. He would jump so high that he swatted the ball away before it could pass through the hoop. In today's basketball, touching the ball after it reaches its apogee is forbidden, but in Mikan's time it was legal because people thought it was impossible anyone could reach that far up high. As a consequence, the NCAA and later the NBA outlawed goaltending.

Mikan was named NCAA College Player of the Year twice in 1945 and 1946, and an All-American three times, leading DePaul to the NIT title in 1945. Mikan led the nation in scoring with 23.9 points per game in 1944-45 and 23.1 in 1945-46. When DePaul won the 1945 National Invitation Tournament, Mikan was named Most Valuable Player for scoring 120 points in three games, including 53 points in a 97-53 win over Rhode Island, setting a Madison Square Garden scoring record.

After playing professionally for the Chicago Gears in 1946, he began playing for the Minneapolis Lakers in 1947, and became the first real celebrity of professional basketball. When the team traveled to New York City's Madison Square Garden, the marquee would read "Tonight: George Mikan vs. Knicks." Many fans came just to see this giant of a man play. Some sportswriters credit him with saving basketball as a professional sport, especially since various franchises and leagues would open and then fold within a few years. Although Mikan often dominated the court, he was not a one-man team. During the late 1940s and early 1950s the Lakers also acquired such outstanding players as Jim Pollard, Vern Mikkelsen, and Slater Martin. With this outstanding team in place, the Lakers went on to win the league championship in six out of seven years (1948, 1949, 1950,

1952, 1953, and 1954). In 1950 the Associated Press named Mikan the greatest basketball player of the first half of the twentieth century.

When the Naismith Memorial Basketball Hall of Fame elected its first inductees in 1959, Mikan was one of the first players honored. He was the first commissioner of the new and short-lived American Basketball association (ABA). During his two years as commissioner, he created the league's dinstinctive red, white, and blue basketball. In the mid-1980s Mikan and a group of Minneapolis businessmen convinced the NBA to start a new team in Minnesota, the Timberwolves. In his later year, Mikan was involved in a long-standing legal battle against the NBA, fighting against the meager pensions for the players who had retired before the league became lucrative. Mikan died after a long-standing battle against diabetes. Since April 2001, a statue of Mikan shooting his trademark hook shot graces the entrance of the Timberwolves' Target Center.

JACK SIKMA

Sikma grew up in Wichert, Illinois, a small Dutch community near St. Anne, which is 15 miles east of Kankakee on Route 1. In his spare time, Jack played basketball using a hoop in his driveway. In the winter, when he couldn't get into the gym, he played in the barn or warehouse. Then Sikma began to grow, and basketball became more of a priority. Between his sophomore and junior year, he grew from 6-foot-1 to 6-foot-5. During the summer he had grown to 6-foot-9. When he enrolled in Illinois Wesleyan, he was 6-foot-11.

St. Anne's 1973 team, which finished fourth in the Class A tournament, expected to field a strong team in 1972-73. It was the second season of Illinois' two-class system, which Jack Sikma and 6-foot-2 forward John Lee were all-conference returnees on a Kankakee Valley team. Sikma was the second leading leading scorer with 100 points in four Class A state tournament games and the leading rebounder with 73.

At Illinois Wesleyan, a Division III school in Bloomington, Illinois, Wesleyan won the CCIW championship in Sikma's last three years and also earned a trip to the Division III playoff in Kansas City. He averaged 27 points and 15 rebounds per game as a senior, was a two-time NAIA All-American selection, was College Player of the Year in Division III as a senior, and was invited to the 1976 Olympic trials. Sikma credits his coach Dennis Bridges as the key to his success in college and the pros. Under Bridges' guidance, Sikma developed low post moves, including a patented inside pivot move where he turned and faced the basket. It has become a maneuver that is taught at a lot of big-men camps today.

He was drafted eighth overall in 1977 by the Seattle SuperSonics. Sikma was named to the NBA's 1977-78 All-Rookie team. Among his main achievements was seven All-Star Game selections (from 1979 to 1985) and a championship ring won with the 1978-79 Sonics, where Sikma teamed with talented players such as Dennis Johnson, Gus Williams and an aging Paul Silas. Sikma never failed to average double figures in points per game throughout his career, and after his stint with the Sonics, he maintained consistent numbers while playing with the

Milwaukee Bucks in his final five seasons. For his career, Sikma scored 17,287 points and grabbed 10,816 rebounds.

Sikma was one of the most accurate shooting centers in NBA history. He holds the rare distinction of leading the league in free throw percentage (92.2%) while playing the center position during the 1987-88 season and averaged 84.9% for his career. Sikma also made over 200 three-pointers during his career with a 32.8% three-point percentage. In June of 2007, Jack Sikma was hired by the Houston Rockets as an assistant to Rick Adelman. Among his duties will be to tutor Yao Ming in "big man" playing strategies.

RUSSELL CROSS

As a freshman at Manley High School on the West Side of Chicago, Illinois, he was 6-foot-6. As a junior, he was 6-foot-10 with a wingspan of a 7-footer. As a senior, he was the most dominant player in Illinois, leading his team to the state championship. Next, Cross opted to play collegiately at Purdue University and for coach Gene Keady.

He was the Big Ten rookie of the year and a two-time All-Big Ten selection. He led Purdue to the NIT finals as a freshman, and sophomore. As a junior, his team lost to Arkansas in the third round of the NCAA tournament. Afterward, he declared himself eligible for the NBA Draft. He was selected by the Golden State Warriors in the 1st round (6th overall) of the 1983 NBA Draft.

His professional career never took off. Cross played in only one NBA season, averaging 3.7 points in 45 games for the warriors in 1983-84. He was slowed by a knee injury that he suffered during his senior year in high school, when a Simeon player came off the bench and tackled him to prevent him from scoring. The injury was never completely repaired, and the knee got progressively worst, despite surgery during his sophomore year at Purdue. Cross was traded by Golden State to Denver but was cut. He played in the CBA, and then went overseas and played in Italy and Spain for seven years. He retired in 1991 after doctors said he couldn't play another year on his damaged knee.

DAVE ROBISCH

Growing up in Cincinnati, Robisch participated in a thriving baseball program that produced Pete Rose, Jimmy Wynn, and Eddie Brinkman. Baseball was his first love, and the sport he played. Later he discovered another hero, Oscar Robertson. In 1965, Robisch arrived in Springfield, Illinois and made an immediate impact in basketball. As a junior, he played with Mark Stoddart, Bill Scheffler, Steve Jurkins, and Jerry Statler. Springfield High School finished 19-12, losing to state runner-up Galesburg and Dale Kelley 69-65 in the supersectional at Macomb. Robisch scored 23 points in the loss. He averaged 23.5 for the season.

Springfield went further in 1967. Robisch averaged 32 points per game and ranked with Collinsville's Tom Parker, Benton's Rich Yunkus, and Marion's Greg Starrick as the state's premier players. Coach Verdie Allizer's team was 30-

3. The Senators lost to state champion Pekin 76-61 in the semifinals, then beat West Rockford 81-65 for third place. In the Pekin loss, Robisch had 41 points. In four games, he scored 152 points, including 47 while beating Quincy 70-68 in double overtime in the supersectional. He had 25 against Champaign Central in the quarterfinals and 39 against West Rockford. His scoring mark stood as a tournament record until 1987. His 77 rebounds still stands as a state record.

Robisch played collegiately at the University of Kansas. He was positioned at center and forward for the Denver Rockets/Denver Nuggets (1971-75 and 1980-83), Indiana Pacers (1975-76 and 1976-77), Baltimore Claws (1975), San Diego Sails (1976), Los Angeles Lakers (1977-79), Cleveland Cavaliers (1979-80), San Antonio Spurs (19830 and Kansas City Kings (1984). He helped the Nuggets win the 1974-75 ABA Western Division.

On October 8, 1975 Robisch was part of one of the more infamous trades in ABA history. The Baltimore Claws, despite financial problems, had obtained the rights to star Dan Issel from the Kentucky Colonels. The Claws were unable to come through with the $500,000 they owed the Colonels for Issel. Under pressure from the league, the Claws traded Issel to the Denver Nuggets in exchange for Robisch and $500,000; the $500,000 was used to pay the Kentucky Colonels the money owed for Issel. In 13 seasons, Robisch played in 930 games and played 22,780 minutes, having a 46.4% field goal percentage (3,997 for 8,620), a 79.8 % free throw percentage (2,587 for 3,241), 6,173 total rebounds, 1,656 assists, 986 turnovers, 2,069 personal fouls and 10,581 points.

KEVIN DUCKWORTH

A 7'0" center, Duckworth attended Thornridge High School in Dolton, Illinois. Afterwards, Duckworth played collegiately at Eastern Illinois University, and was drafted with the ninth pick in the 2nd round of the 1986 NBA Draft by the San Antonio Spurs. All throughout college and early on in his professional career, he experienced weight problems. Later during the 1986-87 season, he was traded to the Portland Trail Blazers for disgruntled rookie Walter Berry.

Due to injuries to centers Steve Johnson and Sam Bowie, Duckworth was pushed into the starting lineup, where he averaged 15.8 points and 7.4 rebounds per game his second season in the NBA. He shot 77.0% from the free throw line and earned the 1988 NBA Most Improved Player Award. The following season, Duckworth improved his averages to 18.1 points and eight rebounds per game, and was named to the Western Conference All-Star team.

The 1990 and 1991 seasons were also successful for Duckworth and the Blazers, advancing to the NBA Finals in 1990, and posting a 63-19 record in the 1990-91 season. In 1991 Duckworth was selected as an NBA All-Star for the second time. However, Duckworth's production began to slip in the 1991-92 season, and was outplayed in the 1992 NBA Finals. At the end of the 1992-93 season, Duckworth was traded to the Washington Bullets for forward Harvey Grant. He played for four more seasons in the NBA, two for the Bullets, one for the Milwaukee Bucks, and one for the Los Angeles Clippers in 1996-97. He retired from professional basketball after that season. On August 26, 2008, he died at 44 of congestive heart failure while traveling in Oregon to host a free basketball clinic.

JEFF WILKINS

Born in Chicago, Illinois, Jeff Wilkins a 6'11" center, played high school basketball at Elgin High School in Elgin, Illinois. Wilkins played college basketball at Illinois State University and was selected with the 15th pick in the 2nd round of the 1977 NBA Draft by the San Antonio Spurs. He signed with the Spurs in July 1977 but was waived prior to the start of the 1977-78 NBA season. He began his NBA playing career in 1980 with the Utah Jazz and spent the majority of it with them. Due to a mid-season trade, he played out part of his final year with the Spurs in 1986. Wilkins played professional basketball in the NBA for eight seasons. He finished with a total of 3,575 points and 2,574 rebounds. He holds career averages of 7.9 points, 5.7 rebounds, and 1.0 assists per game.

DAVE CORZINE

Corzine is a Chicago native who went to John Hershey High School in Arlington Heights, Illinois. He played collegiately at DePaul University in Chicago. He was the 18th draft pick of the 1978 NBA Draft by the Washington Bullets. After two years with the Bullets and two more with the San Antonio Spurs, Corzine returned to his hometown of Chicago to play for the Chicago Bulls for seven seasons. He finished his career with the Orlando Magic and Seattle SuperSonics. A 7-foot center, he averaged 5.9 rebounds per game in his career. His best season was in 1982-83 with the Bulls when he averaged 14.0 points and 8.7 rebounds per game. Corzine is now working as a DePaul radio broadcaster.

JEROME WHITEHEAD

A Waukegan, Illinois native, Jerome attended Waukegan High School. A 6'10" center/forward from Marquette University, Whitehead played on the 1976-77 Marquette Warrior NCAA Championship basketball team for legendary coach, Al McGuire. He was selected by the San Diego Clippers in the 2nd round (41st overall) of the 1978 NBA Draft. Whitehead played 11 NBA seasons from 1978 to 1989. He played for the Clippers, Utah Jazz, Dallas Mavericks, Cleveland Cavaliers, Golden State Warriors, and San Antonio Spurs. In his NBA career, Whitehead played in 679 games and scored a total of 4,423 points.

MELVIN ELY

Melvin Ely was born in Harvey, Illinois and was a standout basketball player at Thornton Township in his native Harvey. Under the guidance of legendary coach Jerry Tarkanian at Fresno State, Ely led the Bulldogs to two NCAA tournament appearances in 2000 and 2001. He also won the WAC Player of the Year award two consecutive seasons in 2001 and 2002.

A 6'10", 225 lbs, forward-center, Ely was drafted by the Los Angeles Clippers in the first round (12th overall pick) of the 2002 NBA Draft. After two seasons in Los Angeles with limited playing time, Ely was traded by the Clippers along with teammate Eddie House on July 4, 2004 to the Bobcats for two second-round draft picks in 2005 and 2005. During the 2004-05 and 2005-06 seasons, Ely rejuvenated his career as a prominent backup.

On October 2, 2006, Ely rejected offers from the Golden State Warriors and Phoenix Suns to sign a one-year, $3 million contract to remain with the Bobcats. On February 13, 2007, he was traded to the San Antonio Spurs in exchange for forward Eric Williams and a second-round draft pick in 2009. In the 2007 offseason, Ely signed with the New Orleans Hornets. It was formally announced on September 12th that it was a two year contract.

ACIE EARL

Earl was a star basketball player from Moline High School, where he played varsity ball for four seasons. Earl led the Marrons to a 23-4 record in 1988, along with future NFL All-Pro Brad Hopkins. Acie was a high school 3rd team All-State in the state of Illinois and ended up being ranked 79th by Street-Smiths Magazine. Acie was a key recruit for the Iowa Hawkeyes, and played 22 games in his freshman season. He averaged 6.0 points and had 50 blocked shots. Acie was a 3 year starter, Playboy Pre-Season All-American, plus 2nd leading score at Iowa with 1,779 total points (first is Roy Marble with 2,116). In his junior year, Acie was *Chicago Tribune's* Big Ten Player of the Year. He is the All-Time shot block leader at Iowa with 358 blocks and holds over 22 game, season and career records. Earl, a 6'10", 240 lb center was the 1992 Defensive Player of the Year.

Acie was the 19th pick in the first round of the 1993 NBA Draft by the Boston Celtics. Acie played 4 years in the NBA with the Celtics, Milwaukee Bucks and Toronto Raptors (holds 5 franchise records). Also for 8 years he played overseas in such notable basketball countries as Serbia/Montenegro, Australia, Spain, Greece, France, Turkey, etc. Acie is currently the head of basketball operations for the Quad City Riverhawks in Davenport, Iowa. Last year he was hired to be an assistant coach for the Rockford Lightning in the CBA. Prior to that, Acie was a head coach in the ABA with the Tijuana Dragones in Mexico.

NAZR MOHAMMED

The son of an immigrant from Ghana, Mohammed was born and raised in Chicago., where he attended high school at Kenwoood Academy. Mohammed entered the University of Kentucky in the fall ot 1995 at a hefty 315 pounds, and saw little playing time during their NCAA Championship season. After slimming down for his sophomore year, Mohammed shared the starting center spot with Jamaal Magloire and was a key contributor in 1997, when the Cats were runner-up to Arizona. Mohammed would once again share the starting post position with Magloire in 1998, and once again they would bring the NCAA Championship home to Kentucky for the second time in three years.

Nazr is 6'10" and 250 lbs, and for his height he has good mobility on the floor. He plays both center and power forward. He is aggressive in offensive rebounding and putbacks. He is consistently a good free-throw shooter averaging 78.5% in the 2005-06 season. After his junior year, Mohammed decided to enter the 1998 NBA Draft. He was selected by the Utah Jazz in the first round as the 29th pick overall. Utah traded his rights to the Philadelphia 76ers, with whom he spent two and a half seasons. He then played for the Atlanta Hawks through the middle of the 2004 season, at which point he went to the New York Knicks. Mohammed split the 2004-05 season between the Knicks and the Spurs (who acquired him in a trade for Malik Rose). He won the 2005 NBA title with the San Antonio Spurs as a member of their starting lineup.

He shared his playing time and the starting center position the next season with Rasho Nesterovic. Afterwards, he turned down a four year contract extension and did not return to the Spurs. On July 4th, 2006, it was announced that he had come to terms on an agreement with the Detroit Pistons and became their starting center. However, after acquiring Chris Webber, he saw limited playing time and was eventually traded to the Charlotte Bobcats, where he's currently playing.

George "Jiff" Wilson

A 6'8"center, Wilson starred at Marshall High School in Chicago, where he won state championships in 1958 and 1960. After playing colleglately at the University of Cincinnati, he won a gold medal at the 1964 Summer Olympics. Wilson was then drafted by the Cincinnati Royals with the 8th pick of the 1964 NBA Draft. He played seven seasons in the NBA with the Royals, the Chicago Bulls, the Seattle SuperSonics, the Phoenix Suns, the Philadelphia 76ers, and the Buffalo Braves, averaging 5.4 points per game and 5.2 rebounds per game in his career. He currently works as a YMCA director and lives in Fairfield, Ohio.

Steven Hunter

Steven Hunter was born in Chicago, Illinois attended Proviso East High School in Maywood, Illinois. The 7'0" center then attended DePaul University and played collegiately with the Blue Demons. He was selected 15th overall in the first round of the 2001 NBA Draft by the Orlando Magic. In the 2005 offseason he signed with the Philadelphia 76ers as a free agent. They traded him to the New Orleans/Oklahoma City Hornets on February 1, 2006 in exchange for two second-round draft picks. On February 10th Philadelphia President Billy King announced that the New Orleans/OklahomaCity Hornets had rescinded the trade that would have sent him to the Hornets in exchange for two second-round picks in the 2006 and 2007 NBA Drafts.

He currently plays professionally with the Denver Nuggets. He's listed as a center-forward and has played for the Orlando Magic, Phoenix Suns and Philadelphia 76ers. He's averaged 5.9 points per game through his career. In 2004-06 he ranked second in the NBA with 4.68 blocks per 48 minutes, behind only Marcus Camby. He usually shoots a good field goal percentage on the shots that he takes as well.

JUSTIN WILLIAMS

Williams was born in Chicago and attended high school at Thornwood High School in South Holland, Illinois. A 6'10", 230 lb power forward-center from the University of Wyoming was signed by the Sacramento Kings to a 10-day contract on January 5, 2007. After the Kings released power forward Maurice Taylor on January 23, Williams was signed to the rest of the season after his two 10-day contracts expired.

He previously played with the NBA Development League's Dakota Wizards, averaging 12.1 points, 12.3 rebounds and 3.08 blocks in 12 games. Sacramento put him on a leave of absence and sent him home to hire legal counsel on October 27, 2007 while traveling with them for an exhibition game in Albuquerque, New Mexico. However, he began the 2007-08 season with the Kings and averaged 1.4 points and 2.2 rebounds in 22 games before being waived on February 16. He subsequently signed a 10-day contract with Houston and appeared in one game for the Rockets. The Golden State Warriors signed him to contract prior to the 2008-09 NBA season as a training camp invitee. Shortly after being waived by the Warriors, the Charlotte Bobcats signed to a contract. Shortly before the start of the 2008-09 regular season, he had been waived by them too.

UWE BLAB

Blab attended Effingham High School in Illinois, and played college basketball for the Indiana University Hoosiers, averaging 16 points per game in his senior year. He earned a degree in Sauerkrauting. He was under constant criticism under coach Bob Knight for not being in good shape.

Drafted 17th overall by the Dallas Mavericks in the 1985 NBA Draft, he never proved to be a significant contributor. His first four seasons, were with the Mavericks, and he played for both the Golden State Warriors and the San Antonio Spurs in his final year. The 7'1", 252 lb center finished with career averages of 2.1 points and 1.8 rebounds per game.

AMAL McCASKILL

Amal was born in Maywood, Illinois and attended high school at St. Joseph in neighboring Westchester, Illinois. After a four-year career at Marquette University, McCaskill was selected by the Orlando Magic with the 49th pick (2nd round) of the 1996 NBA Draft. A 6'11" center, McCaskill played in four NBA seasons with four different teams: 1996-97 with Orlando, 2001-02 with the San Antonio Spurs, 2002-03 with the Atlanta Hawks, and 2003-04 with the Philadelphia 76ers. He played in 114 career NBA games, and scored a total of 204 points, while grabbing a total of 213 rebounds. Amal recently co-executive produced rapper Killah Priest's new album, The Offering.

THOMAS HAMILTON

Thomas Hamilton was born in Chicago, Illinois and attended Chicago's Martin Luther King High School, graduating in 1993. He was a high school teammate of Rashard Griffith (the 38th pick in the 1995 NBA Draft) and the pair led their school to the 1993 Illinois State Basketball Championship. The 7-foot-2 inch, 330+ pound center attended the University of Pittsburgh but did not play on the basketball team. In fact, Hamilton had never played basketball professionally (or in college) prior to the 1995-96 season.

Hamilton was signed by the Boston Celtics at the beginning of the 1995-96 season, but did not appear in a game until five weeks remained in the regular season. He spent most of the season on both the injured and suspended list. When he was fit to play, he appeared in 11 games and scored a total of 25 points. He averaged two rebounds and nearly one block per game in limited action. His weight was listed at 360 pounds when he was taken off the suspended list and appeared in his first NBA game.

Hamilton was signed by the Houston Rockets at the beginning of the 1999-2000 NBA season. He played in 22 games and made seven starts. He suffered a lower back strain and was placed on the injured list for nearly two months until he was released on January 13, 2000. He averaged 12.4 minutes, 3.7 points, 4.1 rebounds, and 0.6 blocks per game with the Rockets.

He was signed by the Chicago Bulls on October 23, 1996 but was released two months later. He was signed again by the Chicago Bulls on October 6, 1997 but was released two weeks later. Although he was signed by Chhicago on two separate ocassions, he never got to play for his hometown team.

CHAPTER NINE

GREAT COACHES & GIRLS BASKETBALL PLAYERS

JERRY SLOAN

He was head coach of the Chicago Bulls for less than three seasons, winning 94 games and losing 121. After Frank Layden's retirement from the Utah Jazz in 1988 as head coach, the Jazz chose Sloan to be his successor. He's currently one of professional basketball's most successful coaches, with a career win-lost record of 1035-689 (as of April 18, 2007), placing him fourth on the list of all-time most winning coaches. Sloan collected his 1,000th career win against the Dallas Mavericks in a 101-79 victory, which made him the fifth coach in NBA history to surpass this milestone. After Tom Kelly stepped down as manager of the Minnesota Twins in 2001, Sloan became the longest tenured head coach in major league sports with a single franchise. The 2007-08 season was his 20th at the helm of the Jazz. On November 7, 2008 Sloan became the first coach in NBA history to win 1,000 games with one team with a 104-97 victory over Oklahoma City.

GLENN "DOC" RIVERS

Following his retirement in July of 1996, Rivers was immediately hired by Turner Sports to work as an on-camera NBA analyst. He also served as an analyst for the Spurs' local television broadcast. Although he enjoyed his work on television, Rivers made it known that he wanted a position as an NBA coach or general manager. Two years into his broadcasting career, he was considered a prime candidate for an NBA coaching position. He was considered for the Washington Wizards head coaching vacancies and the Milwaukee Bucks general manager position, but finally accepted the head coaching job with Orlando Magic in 1999.

He spent four plus seasons as the Head Coach of the Orlando Magic. In his first year at the helm in Orlando, he led a team predicted by most to finish near or at the bottom of the league that included four starters who were not drafted. Rivers guided the team to a 41-41 record, and for his efforts, Rivers was named the 1999-2000 NBA Coach of the Year. Overall he compiled a 171-168 record (.506) in his four-plus season's as Orlando's head coach, advancing the team to the playoffs three times.

He was named to the position of Head Coach of the Boston Celtics on April 29, 2004, becoming the 16th coach in their franchise history. In his first season as Head Coach of the Boston Celtics, Rivers led the club to a 45-37 (.549) record as well as the teams first Atlantic Division title since the 1991-92 season. Rivers guided the Celtics to their 17th NBA championship in 2008.

JOHNNY ORR

During the 1950s, Orr was head coach at Dubuque Senior High School in Dubuque, Iowa. After a long time as assistant coach, including at Wisconsin, Orr attained a head coaching position in 1963 at the University of Massachusetts Amhearst, commonly known as UMass, and guided them to a 15-9 record in 1963-64. Shortly afterward, Orr moved to the University of Michigan as an assistant under Dave Strack, and was named head coach in 1969.

His 1973-74 team made it to the Elite Eight in the NCAA tournament and Orr was named Big Ten Coach of the Year. In 1976, Michigan was the NCAA tournament runner-up to the undefeated Indiana Hoosiers and Orr was named National Coach of the Year. Orr remains the winningest coach in Michigan history with 209 wins and only 113 losses.

Orr joined the Iowa State Cyclones in 1990. The move came about when the Iowa State Athletic Director called him to inquire about Orr's assistant, Bill Frieder. When Orr learned how much Iowa State was willing to pay Frieder, Orr negotiated the job for himself (Frieder then succeeded Orr at Michigan). In Orr's fifth season in Ames, he led the Cyclones to their first NCAA tournament berth in 40 years. The following season, Orr's Cyclones reached the Sweet Sixteen of the 1986 NCAA Men's Division I Basketball Tournament with a second round victory over the number five ranked team in the nation, Michigan. Orr claims this is his greatest victory of his career. Orr led Iowa State to four more NCAA tournament berths before retiring from Iowa State in 1994. He remains the winningest coach in Iowa State history with 218 wins and 200 losses.

RAY MEYER

Ray Meyer was born in Chicago, the son of a candy wholesaler and the youngest of 10 children. He planned to be a priest but turned to sports after starring in basketball at Chicago's Quigley Prep and St. Patrick's Academy, which won the 1932 Catholic high school national title. He was co-captain of the Notre Dame basketball team as a junior and senior, and after serving as an assistant coach for the Irish, was named DePaul's head coach in April 1942.

When Meyer arrived at DePaul in 1942, in his first season, he discovered a basketball hopeful. The young man, a sophomore within an inch or so of his eventual 6-foot-10 inch height, had never played high school basketball. He wore thick glasses and he enrolled at DePaul only after being spurned by the Notre Dame coach because his basketball skills were primitive. Meyer taught George Mikan every aspect of the game and made him take hundreds of hook shots, both right and left handed, everyday while keeping a towel wedged under his opposite arm to maintain proper form. With Mikan playing alongside his 6-7 brother Ed, DePaul won the 1945 N.I.T. championship.

During the 1950's, Meyer achieved a national presence by coaching the college all-star teams that toured each spring playing the Harlem Globetrotters. In the early 1970's, DePaul's basketball fortunes declined. Joey Meyer was captain of his father's worst team, the 1970-71 squad, which went 8-17. But Meyers career flourished in the late 1970's and early 1980's with the arrival of the outstanding players, Dave Corzine, Mark Aguirre and Terry Cummings.

In February 1979, Meyer joined John Wooden, Adolph Rupp and Frank McGuire as the only active coaches elected to the Basketball Hall of Fame. DePaul went to the NCAA tournament's Final Four that season, losing to Larry Bird's Indiana State team, 76-74, in the semifinals. Meyer's teams lost only one regular season game in each of the following three seasons, but never advanced beyond the first round of the NCAA tournament.

When DePaul opened the 1981-82 season against Illinois-Chicago Circle, the Meyer family made sports history. Ray Meyer was coaching against his oldest son, Tommy, in what is believed to have been the first coaching meeting between a father and son in college basketball. The elder Meyer's team prevailed, 78-53. Meyer led DePaul to 20 postseason appearances, relying mostly on homegrown talent. He made his first out-of-state recruiting trip at age 69. When Meyer stepped down, his record of 724-354 placed him No. 5 in career victories among college coaches. Ray Meyer was present for 1,467 consecutive games over a 55-year span as DePaul's coach and as a basketball analyst for the program's radio broadcasts. He died March 17, 2006 at an assistant-living facility outside Chicago. He was 92, but DePaul did not forget him. In June 1998, the university broke ground for a $12 million Ray Meyer Fitness and Recreation Center. And a stretch of Belden Avenue outside the Meyer Center was renamed Ray Meyer Drive.

ARTHUR L. TROUT

Over the course of its 150-year history, Centralia, Illinois, has weathered more than its share of setbacks. The Illinois Central railroad traffic that put the town on the map in 1851 has long since disappeared. Coal mining virtually stopped overnight following a 1947 mine disaster that killed 111 miners. The oil boom, which at one time made the surrounding countryside resemble a derrick factory showroom, dried up in the 1950s. But through good times and bad, Centralia (pop. 14,136) has managed to hold onto a constant source of community pride and pleasure. For nearly 70 years, the Centralia Orphans have been the "winningest" high school boys basketball team in the United States. With a lifetime record of 1,937 wins and 814 losses at the close of the 2002-03 season, the Orphans have celebrated more victories than any other boys' high school basketball team in the country.

The Centralia High School basketball team known as the "Orphans" in 1936 because upstate sports reporters thought them shabby upstarts to be competing at the state level. However, the name became prophetic after the mine disaster; at one time, all the players had lost a father in the mines. Also, the girls basketball team is called the "Annies." Nevertheless, there are some alternative theories as to why the sports teams of Centralia High School are called the "Orpans." One maintains that it is due to a large orphanage that at one time was present in the town, another widely accepted theory is that the players wore a bunch of unmatched jerseys when they went to state and a state reporter said that they look like a bunch of orphans out there.

Folks in town still remember the extraordinary success of the Orphans' brightest star, Dwight "Dike" Eddleman, the team's all-time leading scorer. During his high school years in the 1940s, he was the subject of a feature article in *Life Magazine.* Later, he lettered in three sports at the University of Illinois, competed in the London Olympics (high jump) in 1948, and played in the NBA in the 1950s. Today, the corner of the downtown Centralia Area Historical Society Museum devoted to local sports features a veritable shrine to Eddleman and his accomplishments. Others who rose up into the pros include Bobby Joe Mason, a Harlem Globetrotter for many years, and Dickie Garrett, who played briefly for the Los Angeles Lakers.

The Orphans, formed in 1906, first entered the national spotlight in the 1940s, under coach Arthur L. Trout. Trout truly "made" the Orphans, leading them to more than 800 victories over a 36-year career. Still today, filling Trout Gymnasium is the town's pride. There's usually more request for season tickets than tickets available. The state tournament's most legendary coach may well have been Arthur L. Trout, who stood at the helm of Centralia High School from 1915 through Christmas of 1951, winning 809 career games. He was the first man to coach in four title games as well as the first coach to win three state championships (1918, 1922, 1942). Trout's teams won at least 20 games 21 times, at least 25 games 15 times, and at least 30 games five times. His 1941 squad won an amazing 44 contests and even today is considered one of the Prairie State's premier teams.

VERGIL FLETCHER

Collinsville High School, the Kahoks, named for a fictional Native American tribe, won several Illinois State Championships, in 1961, 1965 (basketball), 1980 (baseball) and 1987 (soccer). Former coach Vergil Fletcher, who was recently named one of the "100" legends of Illinois high school basketball by the Illionois High School Activities Association, won over 700 games in his career. Other famed Kahoks were Kevin Stallings, now coach at Vanderbilt University: Bogie Redmon, also a "top 100 legend," who played on the undefeated 1961 team; Tom Parker, a star at the University of Kentucky after his Collinsville High School days; and Richard Keene, a McDonald's All-American, who played at Illinois in the 1990s.

Collinsville is a city located mainly in Madison County, and partly in St. Clair County, both in Illinois. As of the 2000 census, the city had a population of 24,707. Collinsville is approximately 12 miles from St. Louis, Missouri and is considered part of the city's metropolitan area. Famously, it is home of the world's largest ketchup bottle, a former water tower, and the world horseradish capital.

Vergil Fletcher coached Collinsville to a 32-0 record and a state championship in 1961. Led by all-American Bogie Redmon and all-stater Fred Riddle, the Kahoks crushed three ranked opponents at Champaign, winning by 23, 37 and 34 points. At the time, Collinsville was considered the greatest team to ever play high school basketball in Illinois.

The legendary Vergil Fletcher coached for short stints at Mt. Pulaski and Pana before heading to Collinsville via the armed service. The Kahoks' fourth coach in four seasons, he remained 32 years, winning 747 games and losing only 170 (.815). His career coaching mark was 790-234. Fletcher took a record 14 teams to state, winning two championships. His first was with a 32-0 hall of fame unit in 1961. Four years later, the Kahoks finished their title drive with a mark of 30-2. Fletcher fashioned 20-game winners in all but five seasons at Collinsville, and four of his tournament entries (1957-61) made the state with unblemished records. No one has coached in more state tournament games (34) or won more state tournament games (21) than Fletcher. He ranks in the top 50 in National schoolboy coaching wins to this very day. Visit the Vergil Fletcher Gymnasium at Collinsville High School. In 1983, Vergil Fletcher was inducted into the National High School Sports Hall Of Fame.

MIKE KRZYZEWSKI

Michael "Coach K" Krzyzewski was born in Chicago, Illinois, the son of Polish immigrants. He attended Weber High School in Chicago, before it became a middle school. He was raised on the city's Northwest side. As a high school athlete, he made such an impression he was recruited by coach Bob Knight for the United States Military Academy at West Point, where he became captain of the basketball team. After graduation, he served in the U.S. Army from 1969 to 1974.

During his military service, he coached service teams two years as head coach at U.S. Military Prep School at Belvoir, Virginia. After resigning from the service with a rank of Captain in 1974, Krzyzewski worked as a graduate assistant to his Army coach, Bob Knight, at Indiana University. The following year, he returned to West Point as Head Coach. In 1980, he accepted an invitation to become Head Coach at Duke University, where he has remained. The first three seasons were disappointing, but over the next few years Coach K., as he's often called, led the Duke program through a remarkable turnaround. In 1984, Krzyzewski led his Blue Devils into the NCAA tournament for the first time.

In 1986 Krzyzewski's team reached the Final Four and came within one game of winning the championship. In that year, they had played more games than any other team in the history of college basketball. With the departure of five seniors on the squad, many observers expected a sharp decline in Duke's basketball program, but Krzyzewski's 1987 Blue Devils won 24 games and made it to the Sweet 16, losing to Indiana, which went on to win the national championship.

From 1988 to 1992, Coach K. led his team to the Final four for five consecutive seasons. The legendary John Wooden of UCLA is the only other coach in the history of the tournament to perform this feat. In 1990, Duke again came within one game of winning the national championship. Krzyzewski led Duke to its first national championship in 1991. In the banner year of 1992, Duke maintained the national number one ranking throughout the season, and again won the national title. Mike Krzyzewski is the only coach since John Wooden to win consecutive NCAA championships. In '92 *The Sporting News* named Krzyzewski Sportsman of the Year. He is the first college coach to have been so honored.

He has coached the national team of the United States since 2005, and led them to the gold medal at the 2008 Summer Olympics in Beijing, China. He has led his team to three NCAA Championships, 10 Final Fours (third most in history), and 10 ACC Championships over 28 years at Duke. Currently the winningest active coach in the nation, Krzyzewski has amassed an NCAA-record 69 NCAA tournament victories, while averaging more than 25 wins per season. He has also coached an NCAA record nine 30-win seasons in his tenure. Sixty-one of the 65 four-year players under his tutelage since 1986 have competed in at least one Final Four. On March 1, 2008, Mike Krzyzewski became the 6th men's basketball coach in NCAA history to reach the 800 win plateau. He was elected to the Naismith Memorial Basketball Hall of Fame following the 2001 season.

DOROTHY GATERS

Gaters has won more games than any other basketball coach in Illinois history. Her 33-year record is an incredible 881 wins and just 121 losses. Her teams have won eight state championships and 22 City of Chicago titles. Among her many honors, she's a member of the National Women's Basketball Hall of Fame, and she was named Women's National Basketball Coach of the Year. She is especially proud that many of her players receive college educations by winning basketball scholarships.

A 1964 graduate of Marshall High, Ms Gaters has a national reputation for developing aggressive, athletic teams, and raising the bar for girls' play. In 1974, dorothy Gaters got a job nobody else at Marshall High wanted: starting a girls' basketball program at the city's West Side school. She's turned the program into a powerhouse for girls basketball. Ms. Gaters believes team sports foster academic achievement, an elusive goal at Marshall.

Gaters, a nice lady and tough coach who teaches physical education (she's also the athletic director), attributes her success to her players, and not her game plan. Gaters says that she has not changed he approach to coaching over the years, although youngsters have changed over the years. In most cases she tries to treat each player based on her personality. But she insists that they follow her hard-and-fast rule regarding citizenship. Her players must be aware, she says, that their actions on and off the court have a direct reflection on the team and the coach. In addition to having better basketball skills, Gaters says that she hopes her players leave her program and become better people.

After Gaters graduated from Marshall in 1964 and went to DePaul University. She majored in physical education and figured she would become a gym teacher. She went back to Marshall to do her student teaching and soon after was offered a position at ther old school. When Gaters joined the faculty, the school sought to establish a girls basketball team. No one, she said, wanted the the job of coaching it. Now it may come as a surprise to know that Marshall was not the first Public League team to play in those initial state girls finals in 1977. That honor went to Fenger. But starting in 1978, Marshall won the Public League title 22 of the next 25 years and repesented the conference downstate.

Janet Harris, who would become a three-time Kodak All-American at Georgia, played for Marshall in those early years. The 6-foot-2 inch Harris would set the tone not only for Marshall's future but for other Public League standouts. Gaters first saw Harris while she was in middle school. She worked on her basketball game at a West Side playground. It was a gathering spot for players like Mark Aguirre, Isiah Thomas and Skip Dillard. Harris originally was supposed to attend Westinghouse. But most of her friends were headed for Marshall.

Marie Christian was one of her teammates and helped to win Marshall's first state title in 1982. Now an assistant at Old Dominion, Christian finds it difficult to separate her former coach and her impact on the entire Public League. Gaters' formula for success, developed by following the philosophy of coaches like the late Luther Bedford and John McClendon, helped create players like Kim Williams and two-time Ms. Basketball Cappie Pondexter at Marshall.

Other players and teams have made their mark even during Marshall's dominant span of over a quarter century. Carver's Yolando Griffith, Young's E.C Hill and Natasha Pointer and Washington's Tangela Smith made a major impact in the Public League. It has been in recent years that the rest of the Public League has come close to catching up with Marshall. Young, it can be argued, has taken over the role as Public League favorite in recent years. Girls basketball has grown among the city's public schools, however, thanks should be given to Dorothy Gaters, who agreed to start the club team at Marshall some decades ago.

TAMIKA CATCHINGS

Catchings helped Adlai E. Stevenson High School in Lincolnshire, Illinois to the Illinois IHSA Class AA State Championship in her sophomore year before moving to Texas. Her sophomore year at Stevenson she won Illinois Ms. Basketball (which was at the time was the youngest player ever to win the award). She is a prolific scorer close to and far from the basket, as well as a capable rebounder, ball handler and defender. She became one of the stars of the University of Tennessee women's basketball team. In 2001, she was drafted by the Indiana Fever of the Women's National Basketball Association (WNBA). After sitting out her rookie year due to injury, she had an all-star rookie season in 2002 and was named WNBA Rookie of the Year for that year.

Catchings played for the USA Women's Basketball Team at the 2004 Summer Olympics in Athens, Greece, helping the team win the gold medal. She also played for the USA Women's Basketball Team at the 2008 Summer Olympics in Beiijing, China, again helping the team win the gold meadl. In 2005, she scored her 2,000th point in the WNBA. With this she became the fastest player to score

2,000 career points in the WNBA, reaching the milestone in only four seasons of play. She is also the fastest to 1,000 rebounds, 400 assists, and 399 steals. In 2005, Catchings was named WNBA Defensive Player of the Year. Catchings then repeated as Defensive Player of the Year in 2006.

Catchings is a 5-time WNBA All-Star and 5-time All-WNBA. She was the leading vote-getter for the 2006 WNBA All-Star Game, and at half-time she was announced as a member of the All-Decade Team along with 9 other players and Comets coach Van Chancellor. Catchings is also a leading figure in the Indianapolis community, having started the Catch the Stars Foundation, Inc., which helps disadvantaged youth achieve their dreams.

E.C. HILL

Hill attended Whitney Young High School in Chicago, Illinois where she was a standout basketball player. She attended Northern Illinois University and was a standout basketball player there too. She was a two-time Northern Illinois MVP (1992-93, 1993-94). Hill was the North Star Conference Newcomer of the Year with a 14.2 points per game average in 1991-92. Hill graduated from Northern Illinois in 1995 with a degree in communications.

Before embarking on her pro career, she was named First-Team United States Basketball Writers Association All-America, Kodak District Four All-America, preseason Street and Smith and Basketball Times All-America, Mid-Continent Conference Player of the Year, First-Team All-Mid-Con, and All-Mid-Con Tournament on NIU Hall of Fame coach Jane Albright's 25-6 NCAA Tourney squad that won the 1993-94 Mid Con regular-season title with an 18-0 record, led the league and ranked 16th nationally in scoring (72.0 ppg).

Hill played professionally for the New England Blizzard (1996-99) and Chicago Condors (198-99) in the ABL; the Charlotte Sting (2000), Phoenix Mercury (2001), Los Angeles Sparks (2001), and Orlando Miracle (2002) in the WNBA; Chicago Blaze in the NWBL as well as in Athens, Greece. She's now an assistant coach at NIU.

CAPPIE PONDEXTER

She was raised in Chicago, Illinois and attended Marshall High School on the city's West Side, where she played outstanding basketball. Pondexter attended college at Rutgers University. She led the Scarlet Knight to a 97-22 record and back-to-back Big East Championships in 2005 and 2006. She competed in four NCAA Tournaments, including an Elite Eight appearance in 2005. Pondexter took home several awards, including the 2006 Women's Basketball News Service National Player of the Year. In her college career, the 5'9" guard scored over 2,000 points.

Pondexter was selected 2nd overall in the 2006 WNBA Draft by the Phoenix Mercury. As a rookie, she was named to the western conference WNBA all-star team. In 2007, Pondexter played a key role in the Mercury's championship run, and was named 2007 WNBA Finals Most Valuable Player after averaging 22 points per game during the hard-fought five-game series. She played for the USA Women's Basketball Team at the 2008 Summer Olympics in Beijing, China, helping the team win the gold medal.

YOLANDA GRIFFITH

Griffith was born in Chicago, Illinois and starred in softball and basketball at George Washington Carver on the city's South Side. She made All-American in softball and basketball and still holds the state record for most home runs. In her senoir year (1988-89), she was named in *Parade Magazine's* All-American basketball team. She chose to play collegiately at the University of Iowa, but was forced to sit out her first year of college because she did not meet the freshman eligibility requirements.

After one semester at Iowa, Griffith became pregnant and decided to go back home to Chicago to have her baby. After she gave birth to her daughter, Candace, she attended Palm Beach Junior College in Lake Worth, Florida, where she earned Junior College All-America honors in 1990-91. She later transferred to Florida Atlantic University, which was then a Division II school, where she graduated in 1993.

In 1997, she joined the American Basketball League (ABL). Griffith was selected by the Long beach Stingrays as the number one pick overall in the ABL players draft. In their only season Giffith led the Stingrays to the brink of the ABL title, only to lose to the defending champions, the Columbus Quest. Griffith was named the 1997-98 ABL Defensive Player of the Year and to the All-ABL first team. She finished second in the ABL's Most Valuable Player voting to her future 2000 Summer Olympics teammate Natalie Williams.

After the Long Beach franchise folded after the end of the 1997-98 season, she was dealt to the expansion Chicago Condors, in her hometown. She played there only briefly, however, as the league folded on December 22, 1998. Prior to that, Griffith ranked fifth among league leaders in scoring (17.2 ppg), first in rebounding (12.3 rpg), 19th ib assists (2.6 apg), second in steals (3.3 spg), and second in blocked shots (1.3 bpg).

The Sacramento Monarchs selected Griffith as the 2nd overall draft pick in the 1999 WNBA Draft. She is a four-time WNBA All-Star, and won the WNBA MVP and Defensive Player awards in 1999. In 2005, the Monarchs won their first WNBA title over the Connecticut Sun. Griffith was named the WNBA Finals MVP. She's a member of the WNBA's All-Decade Team, and has become one of the WNBA's most talented and recognizable stars.

CANDACE PARKER

Like her brother Anthony, Parker attended Naperville Central High School in Naperville, Illinois and graduated in 2004. While in high school, Parker led her basketball team to state titles in 2003 and 2004 and amassed numerous accolades. She is the only two-time winner of the *USA Today* Player of the Year, winning the award in 2003 and 2004. Parker won the Naismith and Gatorade Awards as national basketball player of the year during her junior and senior years. She won the Gatorade award again in her senior year to join only Marion Jones and LeBron James and the only back-to-back winners.

She was consensus pick as player of the year in Illinois in 2002, 2003, and 2004. A four year member of the All-State first team, Parker compiled a school-record 2,768 points (22.9 ppg) and 1,592 rebounds (13.2 rpg), while starting 119 of the 121 games in which she played. She also became the first women's player to announce her NCAA women's basketball verbal commitment live on ESPN news.

Parker made sports history in March 2004 by winning the Slam Dunk contest of the McDonald's High School All-American Game in Oklahoma City. Only a seventeen year-old high senior, Parker beat five male competitors for the prestigious title, including future 2005 NBA Slam Dunk contestant JR Smith and champion Josh Smith. The competiton had been won in years past by LeBron James, Vince Carter, and Kobe Bryant. However, there was controversy surrounding the competiton as many believed Parker only received the win because of he gender.

Parker attended the Univesity of Tennessee and ended up taking a medical redshirt her freshman year of college. On January 28, 2007, in a game against Alabama, Parker scored her 1,000 career point as a sophomore making her the fastest player in Lady Vol history to do so. She did it in 56 games, besting Chamique Holdsclaw's mark of 57 games and Tamika Catchings' of 58 games. On March1, at the SEC tournament in Duluth, Georgia, Parker was named the 2008 SEC Player of the Year. On April 3, she led the Lady Vols to their first National Championship since 1998 with 17 points and earned tournament's Most Outstanding Player honor.

The 6'4" forward (also listed as center and guard) again led the Lady Vols to the National Championship in 2008. She was picked 1st overall in the 2008 WNBA Draft by the Los Angeles Sparks. She played for the USA Women's Basketball Team at the 2008 Summer Olympics in Beijing, China, helping the team win the gold medal.

Parker was a unanimous selection as 2008 WNBA rookie of the year. She averaged 18.5 points on 52.3 percent shooting from the field, a WNBA-best 9.5 rebounds and 2.3 blocked shots in the regular season. Among her notable first-season highlights was scoring 34 points in her debut game, dunking in consecutive games, and totaling 71 points in back-to-back wins in July. Parker became the first WNBA player to win WNBA MVP and the rookie of the year award in the same season. Wilt Chamberlain (1959-60)   and Wes Unseld (1968-69) are the only other WNBA/NBA players to have accomplished this feat.

TANGELA SMITH

Tangela Nicole Smith was born in Chicago, Illinois, and attended Washington High School where she was named a 1994 Kodak High School All-

American. Smith graduated from the University of Iowa. She won the 1998 Big Ten Player of the Year award. She was also a 1998 Kodak/WBCA All-America honorable mention and earned 1996 and 1998 All-Big Ten first team and 1997 All-Big Ten honorable mention accolades.

Smith was selected 12th overall in the 1998 WNBA Draft by the Sacramento Monarchs. She played 6 seasons for the Monarchs, helping them reach the playoffs on 5 ocassions. In 2005 she was traded to the Charlotte Sting in exchange for Nicole Powell. Charlotte folded the following 2006 season and Smith's rights were acquired by the Minnesota Lynx in the dispersal draft. On Draft Day in April 2007, the 6'4" forward/center was dealt to the Phoenix Mercury for the #1 overall pick Lindsey Harding. She currently playing for the Phoenix Mercury in the WNBA.

DOMINIQUE CANTY

Canty was born in Chicago, Illinois and attended Whitney Young High School, where she was a 1995 *Street & Smith* All-American and a four-time All-State basketball player. Canty attended the University of Alabama and majored in criminal justice with a minor in social work while spending four seasons on their basketball team. In her senior year, she was named First-Team All-American by the *Associated Press* and the *Sporting News.*

She finished her collegiate career as a two-time All-American and a four-time All-SEC selection, and averaged 18.1 points, 7.2 rebounds and 3.6 assists during her four seasons at Alabama. By the time she graduated, Canty finished her career as the school's all-time leading scorer, male or female. Canty was selected 29th overall in the 3rd round during the 1999 WNBA Draft by the Detriot Shock. She was runner-up in the 1999 WNBA Rookie of the Year award voting.

After playing four seasons with the Shock, the 5'9" forward/guard was traded to the Houston Comets on April 28, 2003 in exchange for the draft rights to Allison Curtin (Houston's 2003 first round draft pick). After the 2001 WNBA season ended, she served as an assistant coach for the Chicago State University's women's basketball team. On February 12, 2007, the Chicago Sky signed her as a free agent. She's currently playing with the Chicago Sky in the WNBA.

CARLA MCGHEE

Carla McGhee attended Peoria Manual High School in Peoria, Illinois where she was an all-state basketball player. She's most notable for her career at the University of Tennessee. She was injured in a motor vehicle accident in 1987 and was in a coma for 47 hours, suffering brain injuries and breaking nearly every bone in her face. She was told that she'd never play again. However, she was a member of the gold-medal winning 1996 Olympic Team. She donated her Olympic gold medal to a community center in Peoria where local kids could see it.

As a member of the Lady Vols, McGhee won two national championships at Tennessee (1987 and 1989) in three tournament appearances. She averaged 6.1 points per game and 5.1 rebounds per game in her collegiate career. McGhee missed her sophomore season due to injury. She was named to the 1987 Tennessee All-Freshman team. McGhee studied sports management.

She played one season in the ABL for the Atlanta Glory, averaging 8.2 points per game and 5.3 rebounds per game in 26 games. She played six pro seasons abroad in Germany (1990-91, 1998), Spain (1991-93) and Italy (1993-95). McGhee was a Spainish League and Spainish/Italian League All-Star in 1993.

NATASHA POINTER

Natasha Pointer attended Whitney Young High School in Chicago, Illinois where she was a four-year starter. She played in the city championship four years and helped her team win the title in 1995 as a sophomore. She averaged 24.7 points, 5.8 rebounds, six assists and six steals as a junior. As a senior, she everaged 25.4 points, 6.3 rebounds to go along with 141 steals, 131 assists and 12 blocked shots. She was named *Parade Magazine* first-team all-American, and *Chicago Sun-Times* Player of the Year.

The 5'6" guard attended Rutgers University and played four years for the Scarlet Knight. As a freshman, she was Big East Rookie of the Year, as well as team MVP and Rookie of the Year. As a sophomore, she led the Big East in assists and ranked 9th in the nation in assists with 6.85 per game. As a junior, she was a preseason candidate for Naismith Player of the Year and for All-America honors. As a senior, she was named a finalist for the Nancy Lieberman-Cline Point Guard award. She was selected as the 52nd pick in the 2001 WNBA Draft by the Portland Fire and was subsequently waived nearly a month later.

ALLISON CURTIN

Allison Curtin attended Taylorville High School in her native Taylorville, Illinois. She was named Ms. Basketball for the state of Illinois after averaging 29 points, 10 rebounds and 5 steals as a senior. She was named first team all-state by the *Chicago Tribune*, *Chicago Sun-times* and *Cnampaign News-Gazette.* She was chosen for the IHSA Class AA all-Tournament team during her high school career. She averaged 22.9 points as a junior to lead Taylorville to a 34-1 record and a second-place finish in the 1997 Class AA State Tournament.

She was named to the Big-Ten Freshman Team and was named University of Illinois Newcomer of the Year. She was selected to the Big-Ten All-Tournament team after averaging 22.3 points in three games. As a sophomore she ranked third in the Big-Ten in scoring (17.5 ppg) and fourth in free-throw shooting (.821). She was named First Team All-Big Ten for the second straight season as a junior, and earned team MVP for the second straight season.

She sat out the 2001-02 season after transferring to Tulsa University. In 2002-03, she was named to the 2003 WAC First Team and All-Newcomer Team. She was named the WAC Player of the Week three times (Nov. 25, Jan. 6, Feb. 3). She ranked seventh nationally in scoring and No. 24 in steals in the final NCAA Statistics for 2002-03. She rewrote eight Tulsa single-season records, including points (692), points per game (23.1), field goals (231), field goal attempts (516), free throws made (174), free throws attempted (207), assists (138) and steals (96) and ranked in the top five in rebounds (227) and three-point field goals made (56).

On April 25, she was the 12th pick overall in the 2003 WNBA Draft by the Houston Comets. She was traded to the Detroit Shock on April 29. She suffered a partially torn right ACL during the 2003 preseason and spent her entire rookie season on the injured list . For her extensive work in the community, she received the WNBA Community Assist Award for July on August 8, 2003 in New York. She finished the 2004 preseason with averages of 5.0 points, 2.5 rebounds, 1.5 assists and 12.8 minutes. However, she was released by the Shock prior to the 2004 regular season.

Cathy Boswell

Cathy Boswell attended Joiliet West in her native Joliet, Illinois where she was an outstanding basketball player. She would go on to become a legendary guard on the Illinois State Women's Basketball team, lettering from 1979-1983. She's the all-time leading scorer in Illinois State history. Boswell scored 2,005 career points, grabbed 1,054 rebounds and holds six school records. She led her team to 90 wins in her career, along with an NCAA bid in 1983, a 15th place finish in the AIAW National Tournament in 1981, and two women's NIT bids in 1980 and 1982.

She was a member of the 1984 women's Olympic gold medalist basketball team. Her other honors include Kodak All-Region selection three times, a Wade trophy finalist twice, a WBCA All-American, JC Penny All-American Five, and a member of four ABAUSA teams. She was also a member of the Chicago Condor in the now defunct ABL.

Pam Gant

Pam Gant is a Joliet, Illinois native and played outstanding basketball at Joliet East High School. She was a three-time all-state basketball player, and she eventually became the first female to earn a tryout with the Harlem Globetrotters. She attended college at Louisiana Tech and was without a doubt the deadliest outside shooter in the history of Lady Techster basketball. The 5-foot-7 inch guard lettered at Tech from 1982 through 1985 and unfortunately played prior to the NCAA's adoption of the three-point line in women's basketball. Her outside shooting prowess was known across the nation as Gant connected on an incredible 54.6 percent of her field goal attempts during her four-year career, including an amazing 57.5 percent her junior and senior seasons.

Gant played on three Final Four teams, including the 1983-82 NCAA National Championship team as a freshman. She earned Kodak All-American honor following the 1984-85 season, one in which Gant averaged 23.6 points a game - still a Louisiana Tech record. She recorded two games of 40-plus points during her career including a career-best of 42 points in a win over Penn State and six games of 30-plus points. Gant currently ranks No.12 in points (1,714), No.10 in field goals made (732), No.10 in free throw percentage (74.4) and No.7 in steals (253) in Lady Techster basketball history.

NORA LEWIS

The Peoria, Illinois native attended Peoria Richwoods where she was a four-time all-state basketball player. She was *USA Today* Player of the Year in 1984-85. Her Louisiana Tech career didn't start on a positive note, but it sure ended up on one. Midway through Lewis' freshman season - one in which she averaged 13.3 points and 7.1 rebounds - the talented forward suffered a season-ending knee injury. However, Lewis would not be deterred. She worked hard during the off-season and responded by averaging 14.2 points and 7.8 rebounds her sophomore season before helping guide Tech to the 1988 national championship game her junior year.

Lewis earned Kodak All-American honors following an incredible senior season that saw her average a double-double with 18.3 points and 10.9 rebounds a contest. The 6-foot forward also earned All-American South Conference and All-Louisiana honors her final two seasons. Currently Lewis ranks No. 10 in points (1,760), N0.5 in free throws made (377) and No.7 in rebounds (1,071) in Lady Techster basketball history. Her No.40 jersey is retired by the school.

JANET HARRIS

Janet Harris was a standout basketball player at Marshall High School on the West Side of her native Chicago, Illinois. Harris attended college at the University of Georgia where she's still Georgia's only four time All-American in women's basketball (1982-85) and still holds the school record for career points (2,641) and rebounds (1,398). Harris is perhaps the greatest performer in a long line of standouts produced by Lady Bulldog basketball.

Harris averaged 20.2 points and 10.7 rebounds during her collegiate career. She led Georgia to a combined 107-24 record during her four seasons in Athens and helped the Lady Bulldogs reach the NCAA Final Four and win the SEC title in 1983, claim another SEC title in 1984 and finish as NCAA Runner-up in 1985. In September, 2002 she was inducted into the University of Georgia's Circle of Honor - the school's highest tribute paid to former Bulldog athletes and coaches.

APPENDIX A

ILLINOIS MR. BASKETBALL

Each year the Illinois Mr. Basketball award is given to the person chosen as the best high school boys basketball player in the U.S. state of Illinois. The award has been given since 1981. Most of the award winners have gone on to play at the highest levels of college basketball, and many have gone on to play in the National Basketball Association. Voting is done on a points system. Each voter selects first, second, and third-place votes. A player receives five points for a first-place vote, three points for each second-place vote, and one point for a third-place vote. The player who receives the most points receives the award.

Year	Illinois Mr. Basketball	School	Points Received	College
2007	Derrick Rose	Simeon Career Academy, Chicago	720	Memphis
2006	Jon Scheyer	Glenbrook North HS, Northbrook	1,187	Duke
2005	Julian Wright	Homewood-Flossmoor HS, Flossmoor	645	Kansas
2004	Shaun Livingston	Peoria Central HS, Peoria	1,056	NBA(letter of intent: Duke)
2003	Shannon Brown	Proviso East HS, Maywood	887	Michigan State
2002	Dee Brown	Proviso East HS, Maywood	952	Illinois
2001	Eddy Curry	Thornwood HS, South Holland	1,443	NBA (letter of intent: DePaul)
2000	Darius Miles	East St. Louis HS, East St. Louis	1,264	NBA (letter of intent: St. John's)
1999	Brian Cook	Lincoln Community HS, Lincoln	903	Illinois
1998	Frank Williams	Manual HS, Peoria	1,049	Illinois
1997	Sergio McClain	Manual HS, Peoria	1,361	Illinois
1996	Ronnie Fields	Farragut HS, Chicago	1,270	(none)
1995	Kevin Garnett	Farragut HS,	1,443	NBA (Minnesota

Chicago Timberwolves)

Year	Name	School	Points	College
1994	Jarrod Gee	St. Martin de Porres HS, Chicago	658	Illinois
1993	Rashard Griffith	Chicago King HS, Chicago	1,329	Wisconsin
1992	Chris Collins	Glenbrook North HS, Northbrook	1,195	Duke
1991	Howard Nathan	Manual HS, Peoria	822	DePaul
1990	Jamie Brandon	Chicago King HS, Chicago	826	Louisiana State
1989	Deon Thomas	Simeon Vocational HS, Chicago	959	Illinois
1988	Eric Anderson	St. Francis de Sales HS, Chicago	1,490	Indiana
1987	Marcus Liberty	Chicago King HS, Chicago	1,286	Illinois
1986	Nick Anderson	Simeon Vocational HS, Chicago	876	Illinois
1985	Ed Horton	Lanphier HS, Springfield	1,735	Iowa
1984	Brian Sloan	McLeansboro HS, McLeansboro	1,303	Indiana
1983	Marty Simmons	Lawrenceville HS, Lawrenceville	2,056	Indiana
1982	Bruce Douglas	Quincy Senior HS, Quincy	1,700	Illinois
1981	Walter Downing	Providence HS, New Lenox	1,301	Marquette

APPENDIX B

MS. BASKETBALL OF ILLINOIS

Year	Winner	School	Points
2008	Sarah Booth	Warren	294
2007	Brittany Johnson	Olney East Richland	568
2006	Theresa Lisch	Belleville Althoff	532
2005	Lindsay Schrader	Bartlett	582
2004	Candace Parker	Naperville Central	1,070
2003	Candace Parker	Naperville Central	805
2002	Candace Parker	Naperville Central	350
2001	Cappie Pondexter	Marshall	728
2000	Cappie Pondexter	Marshall	360
1999	Molly McDowell	Nokomis	640
1998	Allison Curtin	Taylorville	1,118
1997	Courtney Smith	Carlyle	970
1996	Tauja Catchings	Stevenson	1,044
1995	Tamika Catchings	Stevenson	795
1994	Michelle Hasheide	Okawville	779
1993	Kim Williams	Marshall	646
1992	Tammy Van Oppen	Limestone	573
1991	Megan Lucid	Mother McAuley	471
1990	Courtney Parker	Hume Shiloh	560
1989	LaTonia Foster	Marshall	387
1988	Nancy Kennelly	Maine West	420
1987	Cindy Kaufmann	Seneca	561
1986	Doris Carie	Teutopolis	527

Year	Runner-up	School	Points
2008	D'Frantz Smart	Young	146
2007	Devereaux Peters	Fenwick	237
2006	Amanda Thompson	Young	500
2005	Deidre Naughton	New Trier	208
2004	Kassie Drew	Anna-Jonesboro	184
2003	Erin Lawless	Fenwick	524
2002	Johanna Solverson	Lake Zurich	327
2001	Maggie Fontana	Fremd	245
2000	Jamie Schrader	Okawville	334
1999	Olga Gvozdenoviv	Loyola	636
1998	Heather Cassady	Dunlap	343

1997	Allison Curtin	Taylorville	386
1996	Courtney Smith	Carlyle	565
1995	Michelle Hasheider	Okawville	699
1994	Teri Zemaitis	Downers South	592
1993	Amber Law	Carthage	376
1992	Kim Williams	Marshall	255
1991	Becky Clayton	Sullivan	316
1990	Mandy Cunningham	Red Hill	466
1989	Kris Maskala	IHM	334
1988	Yolanda Griffith	Carver	320
1987	Michelle Savage	IHM	290
1986	Carla McGhee	Peoria Manual	309

APPENDIX C

IHSA BOYS BASKETBALL CHAMPIONSHIP GAMES

YEAR	CHAMPION	COACH	RUNNER-UP
At Oak Park YMCA			
1908	Peoria H.S. (17-1)	Les Straesser	Rock Island H.S. (10-5)
At Bloomington YMCA			
1909	Hinsdale H.S. (20-3)	John Snider	Washington H.S. (27-3)
1910	Bloomington H.S. (14-2)	Tom O'Neil	Rock Island H.S. (14-2)
At Bradley Gym, Peoria			
1911	Rockford H.S. (19-1)	Ralph E. Vennum	Mt. Carroll H.S. (13-6)
At Decatur YMCA			
1912	Batavia H.S. (27-2)	K.C. Merrick	Galsesburg H.S. (14-5)
At Bradley Gym, Peoria			
1913	Galesburg H.S. (17-1)	E.W. Hayes	Peoria (Manual) (17-2)
At Decatur YMCA			
1914	Hillsboro H.S. (14-5)	D.O. Kime	Freeport H.S. (17-1)
At Millikin Gym, Decatur			
1915	Freeport H.S. (18-2)	Dan Daugherty	Springfield H.S. (12-8)
1916	Bloomington H.S. (13-6)	E.W. McClure	Robinson H.S, (21-4)
1917	Springfield H.S. (10-3)	Roy A. Wentz	Belvidere H.S. (10-4)
At Springfield H.S.			
1918	Centralia H.S. (23-4)	Arthur L. Trout	Normal (Univ.) (14-6-1)
At Mens Gym Annex (Kenney Gym), Urbana			
1919	Rockford H.S. (23-1)	Frank J. Winters	Springfield H.S. (14-10)
1920	Mt. Vernon H.S. (16-8)	Floyd Stables	Canto H.S. (30-4)
1921	Marion H.S. (26-4)	E.H. Schreiber	Rockford H.S. (18-2)
1922	Centralia H.S. (26-4)	Arthur L. Trout	Atwood H.S. (21-1)
1923	Villa Grove H.S. (23-2)	Curtis Pulliam	Rockford H.S. (19-1)
1924	Elgin H.S. (25-3)	Mark Wilson	Athens H.S. (35-2)
1925	Elgin H.S. (24-2)	Cliff Adams	Champaign H.S. (21-5)
At Huff Gym, Champaign			
1926	Freeport H.S. (19-2)	Glenn Holmes	Canton H.S. (24-12)
1927	Mt. Carmel H.S. (31-2)	Cliff Garrett	Peoria H.S. (22-1)
1928	Canton H.S. (37-7)	Mark A. Peterman	Aurora (West) (20-5)
1929	Johnston City H.S. (29-3)	Larue Van Meter	Champaign H.S. (28-4)
1930	Peoria (Manual) (26-5)	Telfer Mead	Bloomington H.S. (20-4)
1931	Decatur H.S. (29-5)	Gay A. Kintner	Galseburg H.S. (24-4)
1932	Cicero (Morton) (20-2)	Norman A. Ziebel	Canton H.S. (27-5)
1933	Harvey (Thornton) (23-1)	Jack Lipe	Springfield H.S. (22-9)

1934	Quincy (Sr.) (31-2)	Selmer A. Storby	Harvey (Thornton) (34-2)
1935	Springfield H.S. (34-3)	Mark A. Peterman	Harvey (Thornton) (28-5)
1936	Decatur H.S. (24-1)	Gay A. Kintner	Danville H.S. (23-1)
1937	Joliet (Twp.) (27-4)	Herman Walser	Decatur H.S. (23-12)
1938	Dundee H.S. (36-1)	Eugene de Lacey	Briadwood (Reed-Custer) (33-3)
1939	Rockford H.S. (18-2)	James Laude	Paris H.S. (34-4)
1940	Granite City H.S. (29-5)	Byron Bozarth	Herrin H.S. (23-8)
1941	Cicero (Morton) (23-4)	Norman A. Ziebell	Urbana H.S. (22-11)
1942	Centralia H.S. (34-6)	Arthur L. Trout	Paris H.S. (39-1)
1943	Paris H.S. (36-2)	Ernest Eveland	Moline H.S. (24-4)
1944	Taylorville H.S. (45-0)	Dolph Stanley	Elgin H.S. (21-4)
1945	Decatur H.S. (39-2)	Gay A. Kintner	Champaign H.S. (34-2)
1946	Champaign H.S. (38-1)	Harry Combes	Centralia H.S. (29-10)
1947	Paris H.S. (40-2)	Ernest Eveland	Champaign H.S. (33-4)
1948	Pinckneyville H.S. (33-1)	Merrill Thomas	Rockford East (26-4)
1949	Mt. Vernon H.S. (30-3)	Stanley Changnon	Hillsboro H.S. (25-7)
1950	Mt.Vernon H.S. (33-0)	Stanley Changnon	Danville H.S. (29-2)
1951	Freeport H.S. (31-2)	Harry Kinert	Moline H.S. (22-9)
1952	Hebron (Alden H.) (35-1)	Russ Aheam	Quincy (Sr.) (28-5)
1953	LaGrange (Lyons) (29-0)	Greg Sloan	Peoria H.S. (29-4)
1954	Mt. Vernon H.S. (29-3)	Harold Hutchins	Chicago (DuSable) (31-2)
1955	Rockford (West) (27-1)	Alex Saudargas	Elgin H.S. (26-4)
1956	Rockford (West) (28-1)	Alex Saudargas	Edwardsville H.S. (28-6)
1957	Herrin H.S. (31-2)	Earl Lee	Collinsville H.S. (34-1)
1958	Chicago (Marshall) (31-2)	Isadore Salario	Rock Falls H.S. (33-2)
1959	Springfield H.S. (33-1)	Ray Page	Aurora (West) (22-7)
1960	Chicago (Marshall) (31-2)	Isadore Salario	Bridgeport H.S. (33-2)
1961	Collinsville H.S. (32-0)	Vergil Fletcher	Harvey (Thornton) (27-3)
1962	Decatur (Stephen) (31-4)	John Schneitner	Chicago (Carver) (28-5)

At Assembly Hall, Champaign

1963	Chicago (Carver) (28-5)	Larry Hawkins	Centralia H.S. (32-1)
1964	Pekin H.S. (30-3)	Dawson Hawkins	Cobden H.S. (32-3)
1965	Collinsville H.S. (30-2)	Vergil Fletcher	Quincy (Sr.) (26-6)
1966	Harvey (Thornton) (30-2)	Bob Anderson	Galesburg H.S. (27-3)
1967	Pekin H.S. (31-2)	Dawson Hawkins	Carbondale H.S. (29-3)
1968	Evanston (Twp.) (30-1)	Jack Burmaster	Galesburg H.S. (27-3)
1969	Maywood (Proviso East) (30-1)	Tom Millikin	Peoria (Spalding) (28-4)
1970	LaGrange (Lyons) (31-0)	Ron Nikcevich	East Moline (United) (30-3)
1971	Dolton (Thornridge) (31-1)	Ron Ferguson	Oak Lawn (Community) (30-3)
1972A	Lawrenceville H.S. (25-8)	Ron Felling	Mounds (Meridian) (30-2)
1972AA	Dolton (Thornridge) (33-0)	Ron Ferguson	Quincy (Sr.) (28-5)
1973A	Ridgway H.S. (32-1)	Bob Dallas	Maple Park (Kaneland) (20-12)
1973AA	Chicago (Hirsch) (29-2)	Charles Stimpson	New Trier East (21-5)
1974A	Lawrenceville H.S. (30-3)	Ron Felling	Ottawa (Marquette) (29-4)
1974AA	Maywood (Proviso East) (29-4)	Glenn Whittenberg	Chicago Heights

(Bloom) (30-3)

1975A   Venice H.S. (32-2)   Rich Essington   Elmhurst (Timothy Christian)
(27-6)

1975AA Chicago (Phillips) (32-1) Herb Brown   Chicago Heights (Bloom) (23-10)

1976A   Mt. Pulaski H.S. (29-2)   Edward Butkovich   Oneida (ROVA) (28-
3)1976AA Chicago (Morgan Park)   Bill Warden   Aurora (West) (30-3)
(28-5)

1977A   Madison H.S. (29-3)   Larry Graham Aurora (Central Cath.) (23-10)

1977AA Peoria H.S. (29-2)   Bruce Boyle   Springfield (Lanphier) (28-5)

1978A   Nashville H.S. (30-3)   Bob Bogle   Havana H.S. (31-1)

1978AA Lockport Central (33-0)   Bob Basarich Westchester (St. Joseph) (31-2)

1979A   New Lenox (Providence) Frank Palmasani   Havana H.S. (31-1)
(32-1)

1979AA Park Ridge (Maine   Quitman Sullins   Quincy (Sr.) (32-1)
South) (31-1)

1980A   Chicago (Luther South) (27-5) Cliff Doll   Peoria (Bergan) (23-8)

1980AA Chicago (Manley) (31-1)   Willie Little   Effingham H.S. (30-2)

1981A   Madison H.S. (30-2)   Larry Graham   Dunlap H.S. (28-5)

1981AA Quincy (Sr.) (33-0)   Jerry Leggett Maywood (Proviso East) (28-5)

1982A   Lawrenceville H.S. (34-0) Ron Felling   Monmouth H.S. (31-2)

1982AA East St. Louis (Lincoln) (29-1) Bennie Lewis Chicago (Mendel) (29-3)

1983A   Lawrenceville H.S. (34-0) Ron Felling   Flanagan H.S. (30-1)

1983AA Springfield (Lanphier) (30-3) Bob Nika   Peoria H.S. (28-4)

1984A   McLeansboro H.S. (35-0) David Lee   Mt. Pulaski H.S. (29-3)

1984AA Chicago (Simeon) (30-1) Robert Hambric   Evanston (Twp.) (32-1)

1985A   Chicago (Providence-   Tom Shields   Chrisman H.S. (28-5)
St. Mel) (31-3)

1985AA Chicago (Mt. Carmel)   Ed McQuillan Springfield (Lanphier) (29-4)
(28-4)

1986A   Teutopolis H.S. (33-0)   Ken Crawford   Ohio H.S. (29-3)

1986AA Chicago (King) (32-1)   Landon Cox Olympia Fields (Rich Central) (31-2)

1987A   Venice H.S. (29-3)   Clinton Harris, Jr.   Okawville H.S. (29-7)

1987AA East St. Louis (Lincoln) (28-1) Bennie Lewis Chicago (King) (28-5)

1988A   Pana H.S. (28-3)   Charles Strasburger Pinckneyville H.S. (32-3)

!988AA East St. Louis (Lincoln) (28-4) Bennie Lewis   Chicago (St. Francis de
Sales) (29-2)

!989A   Carlyle H.S. (32-3)   Brad Weathers   Rock Island (Alleman) (24-8)

1989AA East St. Louis (Lincoln) Bennie Lewis   Peoria H.S. (32-1)
(29-4)

1990A   Trenton (Wesclin) (30-3) Paul Lusk   Fairbury (Prairie Central) (31-1)

1990AA Chicago (King) (32-0)   Landon Cox   Chicago (Gordon Tech) (30-2)

1991A   Pittsfield H.S. (28-6)   David Bennett   Seneca H.S. (27-5)

1991AA Maywood (Proviso East) Bill Hitt   Peoria (Manual) (31-3)
(32-1)

1992A   Findlay H.S. (31-2)   Michael Reynolds   Normal (University) (29-4)

1992AA Maywood (Proviso East)   Bill Hitt   Peoria (Richwoods) (30-3)
            (33-0)
1993A   Staunton (27-4) H.S.   Randy Legendre Chicago (Hales Franciscan)
                                                            (23-11)
1993AA Chicago (King) (32-0)   Landon Cox   Rockford (Guilford) (27-7)
1994A   Pinckneyville H.S. (33-2)   Dick Corn   Eureka H.S. (30-2)
1994AA Peoria (Manual) (27-6)   Dick Van Scyoc   Carbondale H.S. (28-4)
1995A   Normal (University) (29-3) Cal Hubbard Aurora (A. Christian) (32-2)
1995AA Peoria (Manual) (32-2) Wayne McClain   Harvey (Thornton) (30-2)
At Carver Arena, Peoria
1996A   Shelbyville H.S. (34-1) Sean Taylor   Breese (Mater Dei) (29-5)
1996AA Peoria (Manual) (31-2) Wayne McClain   Harvey (Thornton) (31-1)
1997A   Warsaw H.S. (29-3)   Jeff Dahl   Spring Vally (Hall) (32-1)
1997AA Peoria (Manual) (31-1)   Wayne McClain   Aurora (West) (29-4)
1998A   Nauvoo (N.-Colusa) (32-3) Reno Pinkston Spring Valley (Hall) ((32-1)
1998AA Chicago (Young) (30-1)   George Stanton   Galesburg H.S. (30-3)
1999A   Rock Falls H.S. (31-3)   Thom Sigel   Waterloo (Gibault) (28-7)
1999AA Westchester (St. Joseph) Gene Pingatore   Gurnee (Warren)
            (32-1)   (28-5)
2000A   Pleasant Plains H.S. (34-2) Cliff Cameron   Teutopolis H.S. (33-2)
2000AA Aurora (West) (32-1)   Gordon Kerkman Chicago (Westinghouse)
                                                            (31-2)
2001A   Pinckneyville H.S. (31-4)   Dick Corn   Pana H.S. (29-5)
2001AA Schaumburg H.S. (29-3) Bob Williams   South Holland (Thornwood)
                                                            (32-2)
2002A   Pleasant Plains H.S. (32-3) Cliff Cameron   Herrin H.S. (26-8)
2002AA Chicago (Westinghouse)   Chris Head   Springfield (Lanphier)
            (30-5)   (32-
2)
2003A   Chicago (Hales Franciscan) Gary London   Mt. Carroll (32-2)
            (27-6)
2003AA Peoria H.S. (31-1)   Chuck Buescher South Holland (Thornwood)
                                                            (27-6)
2004A   Chicago (Leo) (28-5)   Noah Cannon   Winnebago H.S. (31-2)
2004AA Peoria H.S. (31-2)   Chuck Buescher Flossmoor (Homewood-F.)
                                                            (31-3)
2005A   title vacated   Winnebago H.S. (30-3)
2005AA Northbrool (Glenbrook   Dave Weber   Carbondale H.S. (31-3)
            North) (32-2)
2006A   Seneca H.S. (35-0)   Dave Evans   Chillicothe (Illinois Valley
Central)

                                                            (27-6)
2006AA Chicago (Simeon) (33-4) Robert Smith   Peoria (Richwoods) (26-7)
2007A   Maroa (M.-Forsyth) (33-1) Chad Cluver Chicago (North Lawndale) (26-10)
2007AA Chicago (Simeon) (33-2) Robert Smith   O'Fallon H.S. (28-8)

APPENDIX D

IHSA Girls Basketball Championship Games

Year	Champion	Coach	Runner-up
At Horton Fieldhouse, Normal			
1977	Sterling H.S. (21-0)	Sue Strong	Washington H.S. (18-4)
At Assembly Hall			
1978	Joliet (West) (29-2)	Jo Streit	Lincoln H.S. (24-3)
1979	Skokie (Niles West) (28-1)	Gene Earl	East St. Louis (Lincoln) (32-2)
1980A	Benton H.S. (25-6)	Sally Niemeyer	Sidell (Jamaica) (23-2)
1980AA	East St. Louis (Lincoln) (31-0)	Earnest Riggins	Chicago (Marshall) (29-3)
1981A	Palos Heights (Chicago Christian) (31-2)	Debbie Ribbens	Quincy (Notre Dame) (28-4)
1981AA	Elk Grove Village (E.G.) (31-1)	Marcia Gordon	Peoria (Richwoods) (30-2)
1982A	Maple Park (Kaneland) (32-1)	Rich Schairer	Metropolis (Massac County) (21-5)
1982AA	Chicago (Marshall) (32-0)	Dorothy Gaters	East St. Louis (Lincoln) (28-3)
1983A	Quincy (Notre Dame) (30-0)	Marvin Smith	Rushville H.S. (29-3)
1983AA	Peoria (Richwoods) (32-0)	Mary Kay Hungate	Chicago (Maria) (28-3)
1984A	Quincy (Notre Dame) (30-2)	Jim Shields	Teutopolis H.S. (28-1)
1984AA	Elmhurst (York) (32-1)	Val Cothem	Peoria (Richwoods) (31-1)
1985A	Elgin (St. Edward) (24-4)	Ken Mattini	Teutopolis H.S. (28-4)
1985AA	Chicago (Marshall) (30-1)	Dorothy Gaters	Wheaton (Central) (29-3)
1986A	Teutopolis H.S. (31-1)	Dennis Koester	Metropolis (Massac County) (30-2)
1986AA	Peoria (Manual) (27-3)	Dennis Brown	Chicago (Marshall) (28-4)
1987A	Seneca H.S. (30-0)	Rich Anderson	Carthage (Hancock Central) (30-1)
1987AA	Westchester (Immaculate Heart of Mary) (32-2)	David Power	Metropolis (Massac County) (29-4)

1988A	Teutopolis H.S. (32-0)	Dennis Koester	Elgin (St. Edward) (29-5)
1988AA	Des Plaines (Maine West) (35-0)	Derril Kipp	Elmhurst (York) (29-6)
1989A	Teutopolis H.S. (31-1)	Dennis Koester	Hume (Shiloh) (30-1)
1989AA	Chicago (Marshall) (33-2)	Dorothy Gaters	Winnetka (New Trier) (32-3)
1990A	Teutopolis H.S. (30-1)	Dennis Koester	Nashville H.S, (29-3)
1990AA	Chicago (Marshall) (27-5)	Dorothy Gaters	Aurora (West) (30-3)
1991A	Sullivan H.S. (35-0)	Scott Thomas	Seneca H.S. (28-1)
1991AA	Chicago (Mother McAuley) (31-3)	Diane Darrah	East St. Louis (Lincoln) (28-2)

At Redbird Arena, Normal

1992A	Carthage (Hancock Central) (30-2)	Dick Biery	Sullivan H.S. (33-2)
1992AA	Chicago (Marshall) (31-1)	Dorothy Gaters	Bartonville (Limestone) (32-1)
1993A	Carthage H.S. (32-1)	Dick Biery	Okawville H.S. (29-5)
1993AA	Chciago (Marshall) (31-1)	Dorothy Gaters	Des Plaines (Maine West) (32-3)
1994A	Okawville H.S. (32-2)	Kathy Lanter	Woodhull (Alwood) (31-1)
1994AA	Glenview (Glenbrook South) (32-3)	Howard Romanek	Chicago (Marshall) (27-4)
1995A	Teutopolis H.S. (33-1)	Dennis Koester	Carlyle H.S. (29-6)
1995AA	Lincolnshire (Stevenson) (33-2)	Frank Mattucci	Chicago (Mother McAuley) (28-6)
1996A	Carlyle H.S. (32-2)	Angie Gherardini	Carthage H.S. (28-7)
1996AA	Lincolnshire (Stevenson) ((34-1)	Frank Mattucci	Elgin H.S. (31-2)
1997A	Carlyle H.S. (33-0)	Angie Gherardini	Teutopolis H.S. (27-4)
1997AA	Wilmette (Loyola Academy) (31-2)	Tanya Johnson	Taylorville H.S. (34-1)
1998A	Nokomis H.S. (33-2)	Maury Hough	Carthage H.S. (33-2)
1998AA	Wilmette (Loyola Academy) (36-1)	Tanya Johnson	East St. Louis (Lincoln) (28-3)
1999A	Nokomis H.S. (33-2)	Maury Hough	Carrollton H.S. (35-1)
1999AA	Chicago (Marshall) (31-1)	Dorothy Gaters	Galesburg H.S. (33-1)
2000A	Okawville H.S. (33-1)	Kathy Lanter	Lewiston H.S. (33-2)
2000AA	Buffalo Grove H.S. (34-4)	Tom Dineen	Chicago (Washington) (33-5)
2001A	Carrollton H.S. (34-1)	Lori Blade	Teutopolis H.S. (28-9)

2001AA Oak Park (Fenwick) (36-2) David Power   Naperville (Neuqua Valley)
                                                                            (30-
6)
2002A   Carrollton H.S. (34-3)   Lori Blade   Augusta (Southeastern) (32-4)
2002AA Hinsdale (Central) (34-1) Steve Gross Chicago Heights (Marion) (31-
2)
2003A   Chicago (Hope) (31-2)   Janelle Spearman   Pana H.S. (32-3)
2003AA Naperville (Central) (35-0) Andy Nussbaum Oak Park (Fenwick) (34-
3)
2004A   Decatur (St. Teresa) (33-0) Bill Ipsen   Hamspire H.S. (30-4)
2004AA Naperville (Central) (33-2) Andy Nussbaum Winnetka (New Trier) (31-
7)
2005A   Rock Island (Alleman)   Jay Hatch   vacated
                        (31-7)
2005AA Peoria (Richwoods) (38-0) John Gross   Bartlett H.S. (30-5)
2006A   Hillsboro H.S. (31-4)   Bret Teutken   Okawville H.S. (29-8)
2006AA Bolingbrook H.S. (31-2)   Anthony Smith   Belleville (Althoff) (33-2)
2007A   Breese (Central) (30-4)   Nathan Reuter   Rochester H.S. (31-6)
2007AA Oak Park (Fenwick) (36-2) David Power   Bolingbrook H.S. (32-2)

Appendix E

100 Legends of the IHSA Boys Basketball Tournament History

- Joe Allen, Chicago (Carver)
- Jeff Baker, Park Ridge (Maine South)
- Kenny Battle, Aurora (West)
- Boyd Batts, Dolton (Thornridge)
- Ted Beach, Champaign (H.S.)
- Dusty Bensko, Pleasant Plains
- Brad Bickett, Ohio (player), Manilus (Bureau Valley) (coach)
- Don Blanken, Dundee
- Lou Boudreau,. Harvey (Thornton)
- Jamie Brandon, Chicago (King)
- Jim Brewer, Maywood, (Proviso East)
- Bruce Brothers, Quincy (Sr)
- Charlie Brown, Chicago (DuSable)
- Quinn Buckner, Dolton (Thornridge)
- Chuck Buescher, Peoria (H.S.)
- Jack Burmastor, Elgin (H.S.) (player), Evanston (Twp.) (coach)
- Ed Butkovich, Canton (player), Mt. Pulaski (coach)
- Ted Caiazza, LaGrange (Lyons)
- Andy Calmes, Warrensburg-Latham
- Cliff Cameron, Pleasant Plains
- Francis Clements, Ottawa (Twp.)
- Jeff Clements, Mt. Pulaski
- Harry Combes, Champaign (H.S.)
- Lynch Conway, Peoria (H.S.)
- Dick Corn, Benton (player), Pinckneyville (coach)
- Landon "Sonny" Cox, Chicago (King)
- Bruce Douglas, Quincy (Sr.)
- Walter Downing, New Lenox (Providence Catholic)
- Mike Duff, Eldorado
- Dwight "Dike" Eddleman, Centralia
- LaPhonso Ellis, East St. Louis (Lincoln)
- Melvin Ely, Harvey (Thornton)
- Ernie Eveland, Waterman, Paris
- Ron Felling, Lawrenceville
- Michael Finley, Maywood (Proviso East)
- Vergil Fletcher, Collinsville

- Jim Flynn, IHSA
- Larry Graham, Madison
- Bob Grant, Pekin
- Lowell Hamilton, Chicago (Providence - St. Mel)
- Dwason "Dawdy" Hawkins, Peoria (H.S.), Pekin
- Bill Heisler, Warsaw
- Max Hooper, Mt. Vernon
- Walt Hoult, Chrisman
- Cal Hobbard, Normal (University)
- Shawn Jeppson, Spring Valley (Hall)
- Dave Johnson, Oneida (ROVA)
- Paul Judson, Hebron
- Phil Judson, Hebron
- Gordon Kerkman, Aurora (West)
- Gay Kintner, Decatur (H.S.)
- Tom Kleinschmidt, Chicago (Gordon Tech)
- Jerry Kuemmerle, Danville (Schlarman)
- C.J. Kupec, Oak Lawn (Community)
- Jerry Leggett, Olympia Fields (Rich Central), Quincy (Sr.)
- Bennie Lewis, East St. Louis (Lincon), East St. Louis (Sr.)
- Marcus Liberty, Chicago (King)
- Richard Liitt, Rock Island (H.S.)
- Jack Lipe, Decatur (H.S.) (player), Harvey (Thornton) (coach)
- Shaun Livingston, Peoria (H.S.)
- Paxton Lumpkin, Chicago (DuSable)
- Cuonzo Martin, East St. Louis (Lincoln)
- Sergio McClain, Peoria (Manual)
- Wayne McClain, Peoria (Manual)
- Jack McDougal, Salem (player), Aurora (West), Rockford Lutheran (coach)
- Tom Michael, Carlyle
- Fred Miller, Pekin
- Doug Mills, Elgin (H.S.) (player), Joliet (Twp.) (coach)
- Dale Minick, Decatur (H.S.)
- Johnny Orr, Taylorville
- Mark Pancratz, Schaumburg
- Mark Peterman, Canton, Springfield (H.S.)
- Andy Phillip, Granite City (H.S.)
- Gene Pingatore, Westchester (St. Joseph)
- Roger Powell, Joliet (Central)
- Bogie Redman, Collinsville
- Quentin Richardson, Chicago (Young)
- Dave Robisch, Springfield (H.S.)
- Chuck Rolinski, Toluca
- Cazzie Russell, Chicago (Carver)
- Herb Scheffler, Springfield (H.S.)

- Jon Scheyer, Northbrook (Glenbrook North)
- Bill Schulz, Hebron
- Jay Shidler, Lawrenceville
- Jack Sikma, St. Anne
- Marty Simmons, Lawrenceville
- Dolph Stanley, Equality, Mt. Pulaski, Taylorville, Rockford (Auburn, Rockford (Boylan)
- Lyndon Swanson, Watseka
- John Thiel, Galesburg
- Isiah Thomas, Westchester (St. Joseph)
- Merrill "Duster" Thomas, Pinckneyville
- Gary Tidwell, Pana, Fairbury Prairie Central)
- Arthur L. Trout, Centralia
- Dick Van Scyoc, Washington, Peoria (Manual)
- Bob Van Vooren, Moline
- Brian Vance, Rock Falls
- John Wessels, Rockford (West)
- Frank Williams, Peoria (Manual)
- George Wilson, Chicago (Marshall)
- Bob Zerrusen, Teutopolis

APPENDIX F

IHSA Boys Basketball All-Time Coaching Records

Most Wins

- **826**, Dick Van Scyoc, Armington, Washington, Peoria (Manual) (826-399, 1950-1994, 44 years)
- **810**, Arthur Trout, Centralia (810-330)
- **795**, Gene Pingatore, Westchester (St. Joseph) (795-263, 1970-2007)
- **792**, Vergil Fletcher, Pana, Mt. Pulaski, Collinsville (792-234)
- **790**, Steve Goers, Bardolph, 1968; Oswego, 1973-75; LaSalle (L.-Peru), 1975-78; Harvard, 1979-81; Rockford (Boylan), 1981-2007 (790-238)
- **779**, Ernie Eveland, Waterman, Paris, Cisne (779-175)
- **754**, Jim Hlafka, Bunker Hill, 1959-2002 (754-347)
- **746,** Will Slager, Palos Hts. (Chicago Christian) (746-286, 1952-1990, 38 years)
- **738**, Dave Luechefeld, Okawville, 1963-2000 (738-347)
- **733**, Bob Dallas, Ridgway, Junction (Gallatin County) (733-387, 1956-1998)
- **718**, Homer (Bill) Barry, Bethany, Forest (F. Strawn-Wing), Huntley, Marengo (718-345, 1958-1997, 38 years)
- **710**, Ron Johnson, Elburn, Maple Park (Kaneland), St. Charles H.S. (710-406, 1957-1998)
- **705**, Dolph Stanley, Equality, Mt. Pulaski, Taylorville, Rockford (Auburn), Rockford (Boylan), Rockford (Country Day) (705-313)
- **682**, Loren Wallace, Nokomis, 1972-75; Lincoln, 1976-87; Bloomington (H.S.), 1989-91; Quincy (Sr.), 1992-2003 (683-392)
- **681**, Dick Corn, Pinckneyville (681-253, 1976-2006)
- **675**, Eugene de Lacey, Dundee (675-161)
- **674**, Chips Giovanine, Bureau (Twp.), Buda (Western), LaSalle (L.-Peru) (674-266, 1959-1993, 34 years)
- **658**, Max Kurland, Chicago (St. Patrick) (658-275, 1959-1994, 35 years)
- **649**, Gay Kintner, Decatur (H.S./Stephen Decatur) (649-299)
- **649**, Chuck Rolinski, Toluca (649-262, 1956-1990, 34 years)

last updated on March 3, 2008

Appendix G

IHSA Girls Basketball All-Time Coaching Records

Most Wins

- **881**, Dorothy Gaters, Chicago (Marshall), 1975-2008 (881-121)
- **706**, David Power, Hillside (Proviso West), 1977-82, Westchester (Immaculate Heart of Mary), 1982-92, Oak Park (Fenwick), 1992-2007 (706-190)
- **677,** Tom Dinnen, Buffalo Grove, 1980-2008 (677-229)
- **650,** Dennis Koester, Teutopolis, 1983-2006 (650-91)
- **624**, Evan Massey, Galesburg (H.S.) 1978-2006, (624-174)
- **623**, Derril Kipp, Des Plaines (Maine West), 1982-2006 (623-174)
- **597**, Nancy Stiff, Arcola, 1974-2008 (597-241)
- **582**, John Gross, Bartonville (Limestone), 1976-2001; Peoria (Richwoods), 2004-2005 (582-168)
- **570**, Sara Rennie, Mt. Vernon, 1977-2006 (570-253)
- **564**, Rich Anderson, Seneca, 1980-2003 (564-80)
- **558**, Carol Plodzien, Paltine (Fremd), 1973-2006 (558-315)
- **553**, Larry Peppers, Hinckley (H.-Big Rock), 1976-2007
- **529**, Mike Deines, Park Ridge (Maine South), 1978-2005 (529-306)
- **522**, Brenda Whitsell, Knoxland, Darien (Hinsdale South), 1978-2007 (522-292)
- **502**, John Nolan, Byron, 1980-2006 (502-208)
- **492**, Maury Hough, Nokomis, 1983-2003 (492-189)
- **490**, Tim Fairchild, Champaign (Centennial), 1979-2003 (490-184)
- **486**, Ann Murray, Centralia, 1976-2003
- **483**, Vicki Green, Rushville, 1980-2003 (483-163)
- **483**, Zeleda Walker, Chicago (Morgan Park), 1976-78, 1980-99 (483-151)

last updated onMay 6, 2008

APPENDIX H

CHICAGO PUBLIC LEAGUE BOYS SWEET 16

The *Chicago Tribune's* Barry Lemkin and Bob Vanderberg pick the best boys Public League players since 1958.

FIRST TEAM

Jamie Brandon, King

6-4, F (Class of '90): The 1990 Mr. Basketball of Illinois, led King to the Class AA title - scoring 26, 28, 27 and 25 points in the state tournament, went on to play at LSU.

Kevin Garnett, Farragut

6-11, C (Class of '95): Current NBA superstar arrived from South Carolina and spent just his senior year in Chicago - enough time to be named Mr. Basketball of Illinois and to lead the Admirals Downstate.

Derrick Rose, Simeon

6-3, G (Class of '07): Led Memphis to NCAA runner-up after leading Simeon to consecutive state titles; the 2007 Mr. Basketball of Illinois scored just two points in the '07 final, yet was the most dominant player on the floor.

Cazzie Russell, Carver

6-5, G (Class of '62): One of the first big guard, led Carver to '62 title game, led Michigan to three Big Ten titles and to Final Four twice; first player taken in 1966 NBA draft.

George Wilson, Marshall

6-8, C (Class of '60): Key man on two Marshall state-title teams ('58 and '60), also starred on Cincinnati's 1962 national champs and was on '64 U.S. Olympic team before going to NBA.

SECOND TEAM

Mark Aguirre, Westinghouse, 6-6, F ('78)

Russell Cross, Manley, 6-10, C ('80)

Ronnie Fields, Farragut, 6-3, G ('96)

Rickey Green, Hirsch, 6-2, G ('73)

Marcus Liberty, King, 6-8, F ('88)

THIRD TEAM

Nick Anderson, Simeon, 6-6, F ('86)

Levi Cobb, Morgan Park, 6-5, F ('76)

Rashard Griffith, King, 6-11, C ('93)

Hersey Hawkins, Westinghouse, 6-3, G ('84)

Quentin Richardson, Young, 6-6, F ('98)

Ben Wilson, Simeon, 6-8, F ('85)

SPECIAL MENTION

(24 more greats to make up a geniune Top 40 hit list)

Joe Allen, Carver; Patrick Beverly, Marshall; Richard Bradshaw, Marshall; Maurice Cheeks, DuSable; Darius Clemons, Phillips; Sherron Collins, Crane; Terry Cummings, Carver; Sean Dockery, Julian; Bo Ellis, Parker; Kiwane Garris, Westinghouse; Tim Hardaway, Carver; Juwan Howard, Vocational; Eddie Johnson, Westinghouse; Ronnie Lester, Dunbar; Sonny Parker, Farragut; Jim Pitts, Marshall; John Robinson, Hirsch; Levertis Robinson, King; Joe Stiffend, Marshall; Deon Thomas, Simeon; Larry Williams, Phillips; Efrem Winters, King; Voise Winters, Gage Park; Michael Wright, Farragut.

APPENDIX I

CHICAGO PUBLIC LEAGUE GIRLS TOP 10

Alan Sutton of the *Chicago Tribune* picks the best 10 Public League girls players of all-time.

FIRST TEAM

Cappie Pondexter, Marshall

5-9, G/F (Class of '01): Pondexter became the first player in Illinois history back-to-back Ms. Illinois Basketball titles (2000 and 2001). She became an All-American at Rutgers, and the Phoenix Mercury guard was named MVP of the 2007 WNBA Finals.

Janet Harris, Marshall

6-2, F (Class of '81): Coach Dorothy Gaters called her "the most dominant player I've ever seen at the high school level," Harris became a three-time All-American at Georgia and was one of three Marshall players to reach the NCAA Final Four in 1985.

Yolanda Griffith, Carver

6-4, F (Class of '88): A *Parade* magazine high school All-American, Griffith's college career was delayed after giving berth to her daughter, Candace. She eventually graduated from Florida Atlantic and has had a major impact since. She led Sacramento to the 2005 WNBA title and won gold medals with the 2000 and 2004 U.S. Olympic teams.

Natasha Pointer, Whitney Young

5-6, G (Class of '97): Rutgers coach Vivian Stringer, watching Pointer as a senior during a Young - Marshall game, said, "I wish I could have her now." Now called Tasha, she was Big East rookie of the year in 1998 and honorable mention All-American in 2000. Rutgers' all-time assist leader is now an assistant coach for the Scarlet Knights.

Kim Williams, Marshall

5-7, G (Class of '93): The high school All-American and 1993 Ms. Illinois Basketball winner helped the Commandoes win back-to-back state titles. She went on to play two seasons for DePaul. Now plays professionally in Greece for M. Alexandros.

SECOND TEAM

Dominique Canty, 5-9, F Young ('95)

E.C. Hill, 5-8, G Young ('90)

Tangela Smith, 6-4, C Washington ('94)

Marie Christian, 5-8, G Marshall ('83)

Constance Jinks, 5-7, G Morgan Park ('99)

APPENDIX J

GATORADE BASKETBALL PLAYER OF THE YEAR

Gatorade Boys Basketball
Player of the Year of Illinois

Year	Player	Position	City	State
2007-08	Michael Dunigan	Center	Chicago	Illinois
2006-07	Derrick Rose	Guard	Chicago	Illinois
2005-06	Jon Scheyer	Guard	Northbrook	Illinois
2004-05	Jonathan Scheyer	Guard	Northbrook	Illinois
2003-04	Shaun Livinston	Guard	Peoria	Illinois
2002-03	Shannon Brown	Guard	Maywood	Illinois
2001-02	Dee Brown	Guard	Maywood	Illinois
2000-01	Eddy Curry	Center	South Holland	Illinois
1999-00	Andre Brown	Forward	Chicago	Illinois
1998-99	Brian Cook	Forward	Lincoln	Illinois
1997-98	Corey Maggette	Forward	Oak Park	Illinois
1996-97	Sergio McClain	Guard/Fwd	Peoria	Illinois
1995-96	Mike Robinson	Fwd/Guard	Peoria	Illinois
1994-95	Kevin Garnett	Center	Chicago	Illinois
1993-94	Antoine Walker	Forward	Chicago	Illinois
1992-93	Rashard Griffith	Center	Chicago	Illinois
1991-92	Ryan Hoover	Point Guard	Rockton	Illinois
1990-91	Juwan Howard	Forward	Chicago	Illinois
1989-90	Jamie Brandon	Guard	Chicago	Illinois
1988-89	Deon Thomas	Center/Fwd	Chicago	Illinois
1987-88	Laphonso Ellis	Center	East St. Louis	Illinois
1986-87	Marcus Liberty	Forward	Chicago	Illinois
1985-86	Nelison Anderson	Guard	Chicago	Illinois

Gatorade Girls Basketball
Player of the Year of Illinois

Year	Player	Position	City	State
2007-08	Sarah Boothe	Center	Gurnee	Illinois
2006-07	Brittany Johnson	Guard	Olney	Illinois
2005-06	Amanda Thompson	Forward	Chicago	Illinois
2004-05	Lindsay Schrader	Guard/Fwd	Bartlett	Illinois

2003-04	Candace Parker	Guard/Fwd/Center	Naperville	Illinois
2002-03	Candace Parker	Fwd/Guard/Center	Naperville	Illinois
2001-02	Candace Parker	Fwd/Center	Naperville	Illinois
2000-01	Cappie Pondexter	Guard	Chicago	Illinois
1999-00	Aminata Yanni	Forward	Machesney Park	Illinois
1998-99	Olga Gvozdenovic	Center	Wilmette	Illinois
1997-98	Dawn Vana	Center	Des Plaines	Illinois
1996-97	Natasha Pointer	Guard	Chicago	Illinois
1995-96	Tauja Catchings	Guard	Lincolnshire	Illinois
1994-95	Dominique Canty	Guard	Chicago	Illinois
1993-94	Tangela Smith	Center	Chicago	Illinois
1992-93	Angie Sapp	Guard	Williamsville	Illinois
1991-92	Michele Ratay	Fwd/Guard	Buffalo Grove	Illinois
1990-91	Jackie Williams	Forward	Joliet	Illinois
1989-90	Yconda E. Hill	Guard	Chicago	Illinois
1988-89	LaTonia Foster	Center	Chicago	Illinois
1987-88	Nancy Kennelly	Guard	Des Plaines	Illinois
1986-87	Micah Bingeman	Guard	Peoria	Illinois
1985-86	Shery Porter	Forward	Chicago	Illinois

REFERENCES CONSULTED

1. http://www.georgiadogs.com
2. http://www.graphics.fansonly.com/schools
3. http://www.suntimes.com/sports/preps/high school
4. http://www.IllinoisState.edu
5. http://www.wnba.com
6. http://www.BasketballReference.com
7. http://www.venomsportstraining.com
8. http://www.espn.com
9. http://www.niuhuskies.com
10. http://www.answers.com
11. http://www.ihsa.org
12. http://www.nba.com
13. http://www.nytimes.com
14. http://www.JSOnline.com
15. http://www.marchmadness.org
16. http://www.ChicagoSports.com
17. http://www.chicagotribune.com
18. http://www.AreaSports.net
19. http://www.BUBraves.com
20. http://www.boston.com/sports
21. http://www.abc.local.go.com
22. http://www.chicagobusiness.com
23. http://www.findarticles.com
24. hhtp://www.achievement.org
25. http://nbrpa.com
26. http://www.americanprofile.com
27. The DuSable Panthers, Ira Berkow, Antheum, New York, 1978
28. Sweet Charlie, Dike, Cazzie, and Bobby Joe, Taylor H. A. Bell, University of Illinois Press, Urbana and Chciago, 2004
29. Glory Days, Taylor Bell, Sports Publishing L.L.C., Champaign, IL, 2006
30. 100 Years of Madness, Scott Johnson, Curt Herron, Pat Heston, Jeff Lampe, Bob Leavitt, MultiAd, Peoria, IL, 2006